Dichroics

Art glass all dressed up

GLASS PRESS

Jackie Paciello-Truty

A GLASS PRESS BOOK

2002 by Glass Press

All rights reserved. No part of this publication may be reproduced, stored in a retrieval system, or transmitted, in any form or by any means, electronic, mechanical, photocopying, recording, or otherwise, without prior written permission from the publisher.

ISBN: 0-9629053-4-8

Library of Congress Cataloging-in-Publication Data

Paciello-Truty, Jackie, 1952-
  Dichroics : art glass all dressed up / by Jackie Paciello-Truty.
      p. cm.
   ISBN 0-9629053-4-8 (Paperback : alk. paper)
  1. Glass craft. I. Title.

TT298 .P33 2002
748.5--dc21
                                      2002151745

Published by:
The Glass Press, div. of Arts & Media, Inc.
10 Canal Street, Suite 300
Bristol, Pennsylvania 19007
(215) 826-1799
Email: info@glasspress.com
Web: www.glasspress.com

For Bulk Purchases and special sales, please contact:
Glass Press
10 Canal Street, Suite 300
Bristol, Pennsylvania 19007
(215) 826-1799
Email: info@glasspress.com
Web: www.glasspress.com

INTRODUCTION

Dichroic-coated glass is fantastic. It is man-made, yet we are continually drawn to it in the same ways we are drawn to a beautiful opal; mesmerized by the play of light across and under its surface.

Like so many other inventions which have become important and integral parts of our daily lives, dichroic-coated glass wasn't created for all the purposes that artists use it for today. Dichroic-coated glass was first developed in the laser industry as a product of interference filter technology and vacuum deposition. It is still used in laser and photographic applications and in theatrical film projectors such as IMAX®. That it has found its way into the realm of creative expression is purely the result of serendipity.

How did we get from there to here? How did we go from reflecting a laser light from the Earth to the Moon, to gazing at a piece of dichroic-coated jewelry in a Michigan Avenue boutique? How is dichroic-coated glass created, how is it used in the Art Glass industry? How does it react to heat, light, and layering? What is the next evolution, where is dichroic-coated glass going and where will it be in another 10 years? This book hopes to answer these questions and many more.

This informational journey is intended to provide insight and inspiration, which are, after all, at the heart of all artistic endeavor. You'll discover that the distance from the coldness of space to the heat of the kiln is shorter than you ever thought possible.

ACKNOWLEDGEMENT

Thanks to Joe and Stu for giving me this opportunity. To my husband, Tom, whose unflagging support and Type B Personality keep me sane (most of the time).

To Gil, Phil, Peter, Joe, Newy, Shirley, Debbie, Jane, Dennis, Gerry, Dan, Glenn, Linda, Leah, John and all the rest who gave of their time, knowledge and inspiration, my thanks. That I am writing this book is due less to an acknowledgement of any expertise on my part, than to my sense of obligation to share what truth and insight I have been fortunate enough to learn from the true experts listed above.

And thanks to all of the glass pioneers of the American Glass Movement, those involved with dichroic coatings, and those who paved the way before. Their passion, perseverance, and creativity have continued to inspire us. Their groundbreaking work has given us the freedom to direct our efforts in the pursuit of artistic expression, and their artwork has set an uncompromising standard of excellence.

Table of Contents

Introduction 3
Dichroics: What, How and Why 7
   The History of Dichroics in Art Glass 8
   The Scientific Explanation 10
Terminology Confusion 19
   Defining a Common Language 19
      Premium 19
      Colors 19
      Patterns 20
      Coding 21
      Transmission 22
      Reflection 22
      Color Shift 22
   Tips to Minimize Confusion 22
Adding Heat to Dichroic Glass 23
   The Color Shift 23
   Crazing 24
   Burnout 26
The Techniques of Using Dichroics in Glass Art 29
   Glass Preparation 29
   Flat Glass Applications 31
   Architectural Applications 33
   Warm and Hot Glass 34
   Torchworked Glass 34
   Furnaceworked Glass 35
   Tips and Techniques 36
      Fused Dichroic Coatings on Clear vs. on Black 36
      Layering Dichroic Glass 37
   Special Effects and Dichroic Coatings 38
      Stenciling 38
      Intentional Crazing .42
The Future of Dichroics in Glass Art 45
Gallery 47
Appendix A - Contributing Artists and Studios 58
Appendix B - Suppliers and Comparative Codings Charts 60
Appendix C - Project: Art Clay Silver and Dichroic Glass 62

Chapter 1

Dichroics: What, How and Why

Trying to discover the truth about dichroic coatings and when they first appeared in the art glass industry is like trying to find the origins of an urban legend. You may have heard any given story many times but you still aren't sure whether there's a kernel of truth in it. There's the "dichroic coatings were first used by NASA to coat astronaut visors" myth. Not true. The coating on astronauts' visors is a gold derivative. There is also the "dichroic glass is made from volcanic ash." I almost believed that one. After all, Mt. St. Helens is located in the Northwest, the birthplace of the American Glass Movement. However, once again, untrue; though glass containing Mt. St. Helens ash does exist. What hurts the dichroic-coated (dichroic) glass industry is that this type of misinformation is being repeatedly published as fact, and general access to the truth—to set the record straight—is lacking. A case in point was an article published about dichroic glass for jewelry in the spring of 2000 in a very reputable and widely read lapidary magazine. In giving a background history, the author claimed that, "dichroic glass was created by using a laser to deposit the coating." There were other fallacies as well, but this basic statement was so far off the mark that it is apparent the statement hadn't been verified for accuracy before publication. At the time this article came out, I was interviewing Gerald Sandberg, owner of "Coatings By Sandberg" (CBS), and he expressed his dismay that, "There is a major problem... most people just don't know. I go to craft fairs and talk to people, and there's a broad variety of 'what is it?' and I go to a booth (where dichroic jewelry is being sold) and they start telling me all this wrong information."

The perpetuation of these fallacies is difficult to fight. One supposed expert tells a student who goes on to teach others and the misinformation spreads like the Black Plague in Renaissance England. I, myself, had initially been informed that there were three (3) colors to dichroic glass, the transmitted, the reflected, and the absorbed (which was actually the reflected, shift color). So, when asked, I merrily passed on what I thought to be sound information. Of course, at that time I didn't have access to several of the pioneers of dichroic art glass production, people like Gerry and Nona Sandberg of CBS, Glenn Brown of Austin Thin Films, and Dan Crow of Savoy Studios. In researching this book and learning the truth, I began to feel angry and embarrassed that I had been guilty of misrepresenting dichroic glass. I can only hope the information in this book will be a restitution, of sorts.

THE HISTORY OF DICHROICS IN ART GLASS *(sort of)*

As is true with many histories, there was no single, defining moment, no big, black, monolith ("...my God. It's full of stars!") that heralded the instant dichroic glass made the leap from aerospace filter to art form. Although everyone with whom I spoke was in agreement that the West Coast was where that leap was made. According to Gerry Sandberg, of CBS Coatings, one of the first artists to be exposed to dichroics was Murray Schwartz. Gerry was working at GM Vacuum Coatings, which was producing dichroic glass filters. Murray came into GM and bought some scrap pieces that had color but were rejected by GM. He cut the glass into 1" squares pieces and sold them to other artists at craft fairs. Linda Abbott, a glass and wire artist and author, remembers begging a piece from "some aerospace guys" who ran a small glass studio in Venice, California in the mid-70s. Gil Reynolds, artist and author, says he was at Corning Glassworks, in New York in the mid-1980s, and found a broken, dichroic projector bulb. He took the pieces.

One of the first distributors of dichroics for artists was Allen Graef. He was working out of Long Beach, California, was artist-trained, and owned a glass beveling business. In the mid-'80s, Allen came to GM seeking to market dichroic glass to the art community. They struck a deal. When the vacuum chambers were available, GM would coat glass with specific colors, and Graef would sell it.

In 1988, Dennis Schmidt, whose background was in physics, started a company out of Portland, Oregon called Thin Layer Coatings (TLC). They produced dichroic lamp filters for the dental industry, and other technical applications. TLC spent a great deal of time and money in research and development to reconfigure their formulae and chambers to produce dichroic coatings for the art community. Unfortunately, as Dennis tells it, TLC put so much of its resources into these first years that, by 1995, the company had exhausted itself and could no longer remain viable. Dennis, along with his wife and daughter, run a studio called Pyromania, and produce dichroic coatings for themselves and a few select artists.

In the '80s, a company called OCLI (Optical Coating Lab Industries) was the largest optical coating house in the country. They decided to begin producing dichroic–coated glass for the art industry, and put up a $10,000 prize for an art object made with their glass. In 1990 they approached Peter McGrain to create a showpiece using their glass. He created 2 small, autonomous panels, one of which is shown in Chapter Four. OCLI discovered rather quickly, however, that existing demand in the art glass industry was very small. Soon after, they dropped their production of coated art glass.

Enter Glenn Brown, who was already involved in the vacuum coating business. When OCLI stopped producing for the art community Glenn saw a business opportunity and stepped in. The late 1980s and early 1990s saw the beginning of Austin Thin Films, and DichroMagic. Brown sold through existing art glass distributors, and as glass artists began to discover dichroic glass, demand increased.

Initially, most dichroic glass was 1mm float glass. It was cut into pieces which were foiled for suncatchers or cut into strips and hung on rings and earrings. The information I gathered suggests that one of the first people to fuse dichroic glass was Murray Schwartz' wife, who had worked with Bullseye during the time they were developing their Tested Compatible system. Imagine the surprise within the art glass community when it was discovered that this incredible, colored coating wouldn't immediately disappear when it was fired. Not only did the coatings survive firing, they developed whole new sets of characteristics. Word spread very quickly. Allen Graef began distributing dichroic glass to fusing artists as well.

Remember GM Vacuum Coatings? Gerry Sandberg was still selling dichroic glass to artists, but only on a small scale, and without any specific marketing efforts. GM specialized in technical coatings and, like the other companies that continued to produce dichroic glass for the optical and aerospace industry, they were reluctant to increase production in art glass coatings. Production of art glass coatings meant less chamber time for the higher profit technical orders. A company like GM could make a hot-coated mirror for IMAX® and sell it for $250, or in the same amount of time, they could make an art coating which could sell for $70.

As small as the market for coated art glass was initially, demand soon began to exceed the capacity of its manufacturers. At that time GM Vacuum Coatings, Thin Layer Coatings and Austin Thin Films were all producing dichroic glass for the art market. Yet, there was a 6 month backlog in production, and there simply wasn't enough production capacity available to manufacture all the coated glass that was needed. The art glass market was not happy. Artists couldn't get the coated glass they wanted, delivery times were inconsistent, uniformity and quality of coatings were unpredictable, and there were major problems with the coatings burning out. There was some limited communication between distributors and artists, but very little information was being made available on how to properly use dichroic glass. Those artists brave and bold enough to play around and experiment with this expensive glass began to figure out how to use it and fuse it to make jewelry.

Enter Savoy Studios, a fine art glass studio in Oregon. When TLC closed in 1995, Dennis Schmidt helped install a vacuum deposition chamber at Savoy which, until recently, created dichroic art glass exclusively for its own work. As of 2001, however, Savoy Studios has become a direct distributor of their coated glass to the glass art community.

In 1998, Gerry Sandberg found he couldn't get enough chamber time at GM to meet the art glass demands. After a failed attempt to purchase GM Vacuum Coatings, he determined the time was right, left GM, and started Coatings by Sandberg (CBS). There was such a high demand for dichroic art glass that Sandberg found himself with orders even before his vacuum chambers were built. In December of 2000, CBS moved their facilities to larger quarters 5 miles from their original factory. Austin Thin Films moved to larger quarters in 2000 as well.

Until very recently, dichroic coatings were strongly associated with the glass manufacturers Bullseye, Uroboros, and Moretti. In the year 2000, Spectrum Glass introduced a line of fusing glass, which became available to the art glass community with dichroic coatings very soon after.

There are probably those who would dispute some of this timeline I've developed. I admit that it's impossible to fit all of the incredible events of the last two decades into a few paragraphs. What I wanted to impart was some sense of the frenzy of creative energy that burst onto the art glass scene with the coming of dichroic coatings to the West Coat. The discovery of the suitability of dichroics for glass art made an immediate and permanent impact on this ancient craft.

The biggest dispute of all may be over the correct way to refer to dichroic glass. I am loath to use the term dichroic glass and will attempt to refrain from it in these pages, as it is a misnomer. It perpetuates the myth that dichroic glass is an entity unto itself, that the substrate glass is somehow imbued with special powers that cannot be separated from the dichroic coating.

THE SCIENTIFIC EXPLANATION

I considered long and hard the question of whether it was essential to include the scientific explanation of dichroic coatings or not; whether defining it would contribute to glass artists' ultimate understanding and control of the creative process, or just muddy the waters. I came to the conclusion that using and controlling dichroic glass would be much more difficult without a basic understanding of its origins. How does it do what it does and what is the science behind it?

First and foremost, the dichroic coating, in and of itself, is colorless. The coating creates a selective barrier between the light radiating from a source, and the light which our eyes perceive. This gives us the term: interference filter technology.

Going back to high school science class, you should remember that we humans perceive light within a narrow spectrum of wavelengths and their corresponding colors. When white light is shone through a prism, it is broken up into the colors of the spectrum: violet, blue, green, yellow, orange and red. Each color represents a specific wavelength of light, measured in nanometers (1 millionth of a meter). At the bottom of the spectrum, the violet range, the wavelength is approximately .400 nm (nanometers). At the top of the spectrum, the red range, the wavelength is approximately .800 nm. Remember, this is only the light that the human eye can perceive. There are also the ultraviolet, infrared, x-ray, gamma ray and other 'invisible' wavelengths.

visual spectrum

400 nm   800 nm

Figure 1

FIGURE 1
HUMAN VISUAL LIGHT SPECTRUM

It is important to remember that when we see a red chair, what we are actually perceiving are the remains of the white light that has struck the chair. The red wavelengths are reflected to our eyes, while the chair absorbs all the other wavelengths. To see white, all of the wavelengths are reflected, to see black, none are reflected.

The above example considers only reflection and absorption. When we talk about glass, we also must consider "transmission." This refers to the light that passes through the object to our eyes. It is this transmitted light that is important to our understanding of how dichroic glass coatings work.

At first, scientists were attempting to find a substance which, when coated onto a smooth surface, would cause 99% or more of the light-waves to be reflected. This substance would be used in conjunction with lasers to maximize the intensity and power of a laser beam. In essence, they were creating a mirror. The first dichroic mirror used in an artistic application, most likely, was a cyan (blue) /red mirror, intended for a helium/neon laser. Technically then, when we look at a cyan/red piece of dichroic glass, we are also looking at a helium/neon laser mirror! In IMAX® theater projectors, this same filter technology is used in what are known as "hot and cold mirrors," the purpose of which is to siphon off heat and keep the film cool (*figure 2*). The cold mirror has a silvery coating that reflects all visual light and transmits infrared. It is placed in the projector at a 45-degree angle. When the total light energy hits the mirror, the visual light is reflected off at a 45-degree angle, and the infrared energy (which is heat) is transmitted

Dichroics

FIGURE 2
HOT MIRROR/
COLD MIRROR

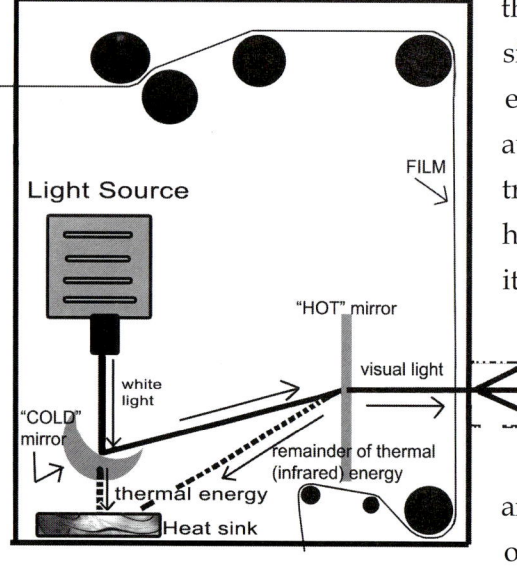

Figure 2

FIGURE 3
PRODUCTION
CHAMBER
INTERIOR.
DIAGRAM
FROM
GM LABS

Figure 3

through the coating to a water-cooled heat sink and is carried away. The visual light energy, which has already been reflected away from the heat of the infrared, is now transmitted through another mirror, the hot mirror. This mirror does the opposite: it transmits the visual light (to the film gate) and reflects any remaining infrared light back into the heat sink and away from the film. Therefore, you end up with all the light energy, and none of the dangerous heat that would otherwise burn out the film.

There is much more to it, of course, but these are the basics, which should provide a foundation for the understanding of dichroic coatings.

Dichroic coatings are sought in the technical industries for the functions they perform. The color of any given filter is totally irrelevant to the scientists creating the coating. The coating must perform as an interference filter, the fact that it may or may not be "pretty" is of no consequence. Once artists discovered the unique beauty of dichroic coatings, however, the opposite became true. For artists, a coating's use as a filter was subordinate to the visible colors created in its manufacture. It wasn't long before artists began to demand glass whose coatings reflected or transmitted very specific colors. This is where an understanding of the true nature of dichroic coatings becomes essential.

As mentioned previously, the coatings themselves are colorless. They are composed of certain oxides, titanium, zirconium and others, but they are not considered metals. Instead, they are called dielectrics, despite the fact that they are actually insulators and do not conduct electricity at all. These oxides are placed in a chamber, out of which as much air as is technically possible is removed by vacuum pumps. In the chambers used at Coatings by Sandberg (*Photo 1*), the oxide source is placed in the center at the bottom of the chamber. Sheets of glass are then suspended from fixed positions on the ceiling of the chamber. The oxides are then superheated, creating a vapor which deposits itself on the surface of the glass. This technology is called vacuum deposition. The glass acts as a substrate for the dichroic layer.

Since a near total vacuum exists inside the chamber, superheated molecules of the molten oxides leave the vapor, radiating in straight lines. Without the interference of other molecules (air, pollution, other contaminants) there is nothing to impede their path. They strike the glass surface and adhere, creating a crystal structure on the glass.

At first, the layer is negligible, and barely interferes with the transmission of light. But, as more layers are deposited, the color begins to intensify. The more layers, the more intense the color. The number of layers has no effect on hue, only on color saturation. Each specific transmitted color is the result of a particular pattern of high refractive index and low refractive index substances. Refractive index, simplified, refers to the degree to which the light is bent, or refracted. Like when you put a spoon in a glass of water and see how the spoon appears to bend at the point where it enters the water. The low refractive index substance is usually quartz. The high refractive index substance is a chosen metal oxide. This "stack" of the high index/low index vapors released on the substrate is repeated over and over, in layers, building up one after the other, anywhere from 10 to 15 or more. (*See photo 2*) The result is a coating that transmits a particular wavelength of light (primary color), and reflects all of the rest (reflected color).

Important Fact: the transmitted and reflected colors are inseparably tied together. You can control one, but not without affecting the other. Example: If you have a piece of dichroic clear glass whose transmitted color is a pale green,

PHOTO 1
PRODUCTION CHAMBER AT COATINGS BY SANDBERG

PHOTO 2
GREEN TRANSMISSION, MAGENTA REFLECTION - DICHROIC GLASS

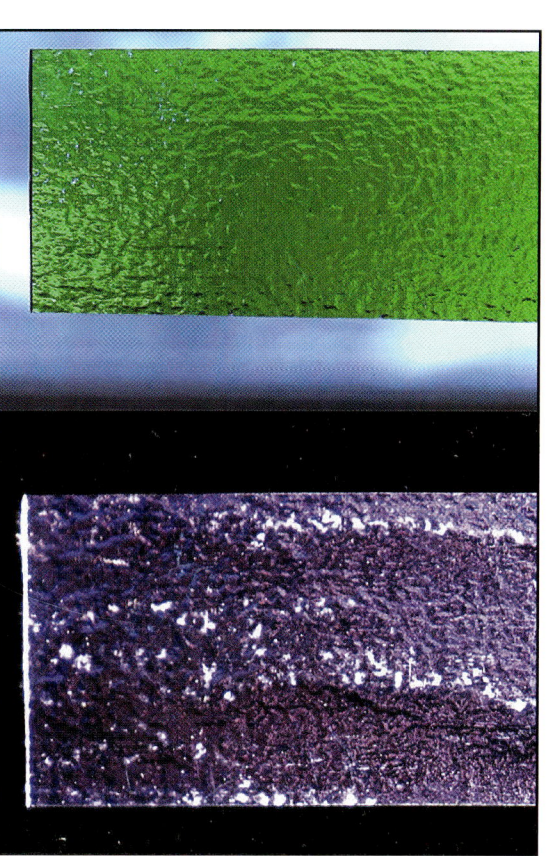

Photo 2

Chapter 1

13

its reflected color must be a bright magenta. Why? Look at the figure 5 on page 20. If you transmit all of the green wavelengths, and only the green wavelengths, then all that remains of the spectrum are the blue and red wavelengths. These combine to make magenta. Now, if you narrow the wavelength of the green, resulting in a brighter, purer green, then its reflected color will be more of a paler pink. In other words, you only have so much energy to play with. If you concentrate the focus of the energy on the transmitted color, you will have less energy left for the reflected color.

The next important point to discuss is the shift color, and what causes it. The shift color is the color that is perceived when a piece of dichroic glass is held at a 45-degree angle. For instance, if you take a piece of dichroic glass with a teal (blue-green) reflection and hold it at an angle, the color shifts to blue. If you hold a piece of copper (dark red) reflected dichroic glass, the color shifts to green/gold. The color will always shift "down" the spectrum, towards the blue/violet. Dark red will shift lighter, toward the orange; blue/violet will shift darker, toward the violet and may even shift off the visual spectrum altogether. Why? There is a complicated explanation that has to do with the change in the light waves that are reflected off of the 45 degree surface. But the answer also involves several other factors (explained by complex, mathematical models) that, together, result in the "appearance" of a thinner coating, which explains the color shift toward the violet.

PHOTO 3
SAME PIECE OF DICHROIC GLASS WITH REFLECTED LIGHT, AND THEN SHIFT COLOR CHANGE.

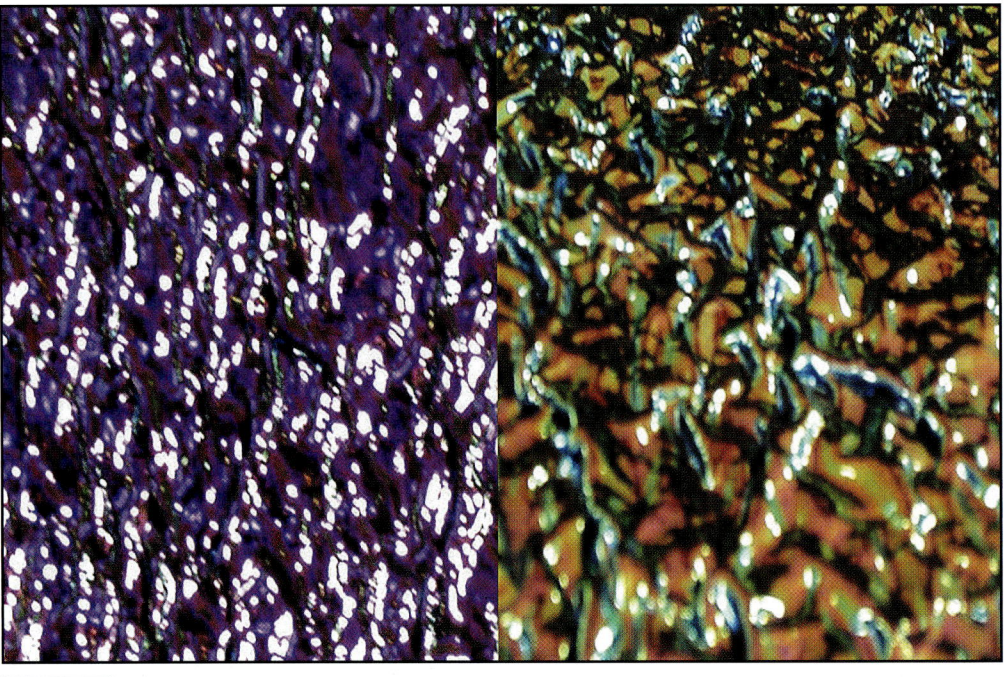

Photo 3

This property is also important to remember when examining a sheet of dichroic glass. Returning to the production process and *figure 2*, we spoke of the sheets of clear or black glass being suspended inside a vacuum chamber.

The molecules of molten oxides radiate out from the central source. Because the vacuum has eliminated any interference in their paths, the molecules continue moving in straight lines until they hit the glass.

However, since you're depositing at a rate of about 1000 angstroms/second, as the molecules move out from the source, they're traveling further, and taking longer to reach the surface of the glass. As a result of having the oxide release from a central source, the layer will necessarily be thinner at the perimeter of the glass. If the glass remains stationary in the chamber, the result is a flat sheet of glass with the thickest layer in the center, (the shortest distance from the source) and radiating concentric circles in ever-decreasing thickness toward the outside. And since color is directly proportional to thickness, the glass appears to be a rainbow tinted bulls-eye, deep red in the center to blue/violet at the edge. Unfortunately (or fortunately, depending on your perspective), colors can be much more difficult to control if the substrate glass has texture. If you can, imagine a deep ripple or granite glass, full of peaks, troughs, hills and valleys, all of varying depths and angles. From what we've already learned about how dichroic coatings are applied, we know that the thickness of each layer varies as a function of the distance from the vapor source. Distance also increases the angle at which the vapor molecules hit the glass. Now, visualize that sheet of ripple glass again. The dichroic coating is going to hit various points on the sheet at different distances, but it's also going to hit the peaks and valleys unevenly, creating different thicknesses. The resulting coated sheet may be a gorgeous, mind-bending array of colors, which includes the intended primary reflected color. However, it will also appear to reflect shift colors; those toward the blue/violet end of the spectrum, and everything in between. When trying to find the primary reflected color on clear, textured, coated glass, first identify the transmitted color. Knowing the fixed and predictable relationship between transmitted and reflected colors will point you in the right direction. And, knowing the direction of the dichroic color shifts should provide the clues needed to determine the reflected color. If the coating is on textured black glass, you have to identify the primary reflected color. To do that, look straight down at

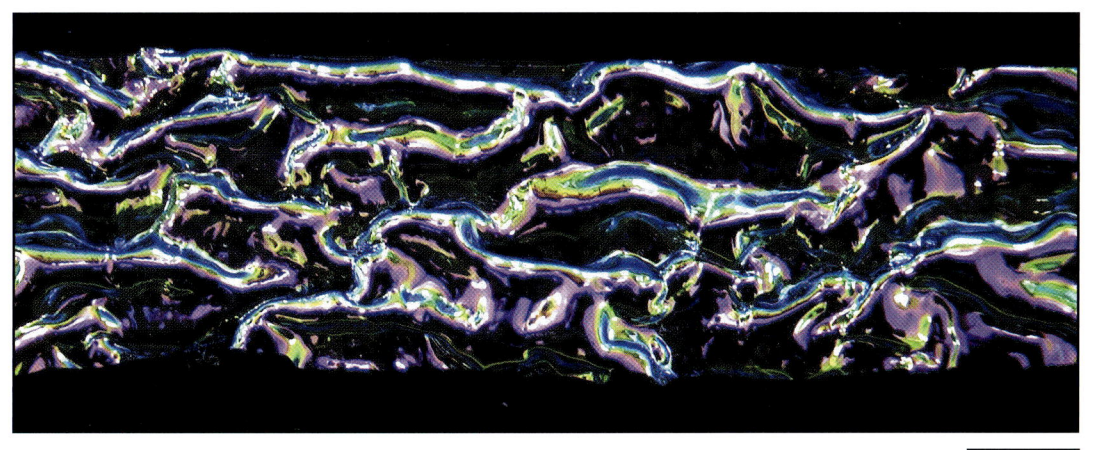

Photo 4

PHOTO 4
TEXTURED DICHROIC ON BLACK GLASS

the glass and identify the highest points on the glass. There should be one, distinct color among the various shift colors. That will be your primary reflected color. Remember that any dichroic coating on black glass will ONLY have a reflected color. Light cannot transmit through the black glass.

There is one important question to consider: If the dichroic coating hits the glass at different distances and angles at different times (*refer to figure 3*), and if thickness of the coating determines color, then how do manufacturers achieve uniform color throughout any particular sheet of glass? The answer is to rotate the glass within the chamber. Each individual sheet rotates above the molten source, and, all of the suspended sheets rotate within the chamber itself. The timing of the rotation is crucial, because the particles that make up the coating need to reach the entire surface of the glass with the same depth and uniformity. If the thickness of the coating varies as little as 7% over any part of the glass, the result may be an entire color variance. This is why, if color uniformity is not well controlled, you may see the center of a sheet of dichroic to be teal, while the outside edges have shifted all the way to blue. Uniformity of color is a significant factor when considering the quality of the dichroic coating. This is especially true if the artist needs to yield a consistent color from every square inch of the sheet. Each manufacturer has its own formula, its own recipe for achieving uniformity of color. According to one manufacturer, however, perfect uniformity is only possible if a manufacturer is willing to invest time and money in quality control. Speed of rotation, rate of deposition, temperature of the substrate (glass) and distance from the source (metallic oxide) to the substrate are a few variables that will affect uniformity of color across any one sheet of dichroic glass.

<u>Reflection versus Transmission</u>: Why can't we get a purple transmitter with an orange reflector?

Understanding the relationship between the reflected and the transmitted color in dichroic glass is absolutely essential. As stated before, the two are inextricably tied together and one cannot be controlled without affecting the other.

In the early days of dichroic art glass, the first coatings created intentionally were: yellow/blue, magenta/green, blue/gold, cyan/red, where the first color is the transmitted color and the second is the reflected (which is how most manufacturing companies list them). If you examine the reflected colors in this list, you will still see the basic colors of the rainbow: violet, blue, green, yellow and red. The transmitted colors create a secondary rainbow: yellow, magenta, blue and cyan. Initially, companies were concerned only with the reflected color, knowing that the transmitted color was a foregone conclusion. In other words, creating yellow/blue meant laying a stack of oxides that would reflect a strong, blue wavelength energy and transmit all the rest. The result of the remaining wavelength energy created a pale yellow.

What the glass artist needs to keep in mind is that there is a finite amount of light energy to manipulate. All other factors being equal, the more energy reflected, the less energy transmitted. Conversely, the more energy transmitted, the less available to the reflected color. This energy only refers to saturation, or intensity of color, not the hue, or the color itself. Going back once again to the graph, in order to get a red/silver, you have to reflect nearly all of the energy, producing a near-mirror finish. That's the silver. There's practically no transmission. If, however, you shift the stack down the spectrum just a little, so that some reds are filtering through, then the silver will be less intense, and a pale red will begin to be transmitted through the glass. In figure 4 you will see an example of how a magenta/green coating looks in a basic wavelength curve. The middle of the color wavelength spectrum, near 550 nanometers, is green. If you create a stack which reflects a strong green, then all the rest of the energy, mainly blues and reds, will be transmitted through the glass. Red and blue make purple or, in this case, magenta.

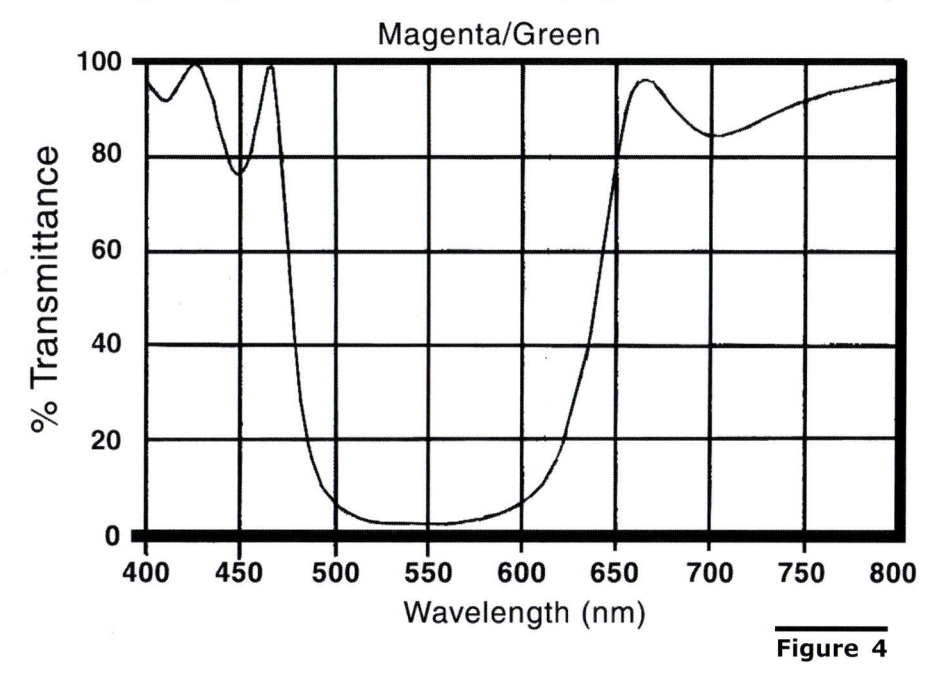

FIGURE 4
MAGENTA/
GREEN
SPECTROGRAPH

Figure 4

The relationship between the reflected and the transmitted colors is based on physical laws. You can manipulate the wavelengths, create multiple stacks which fool the eye, but the physics remains the same.

This leads to another question. What if we want a specific reflected color? Say, for instance, a nice emerald green? Can it be specially created? What about a salmon color, or the blue in an Arizona sunrise? The answer is, yes. Theoretically, any color can be created as a reflected color. And, for one company currently manufacturing dichroic art glass, it's a matter of routine to take special orders from glass artists in need of very specific colors. They call them "premium" colors or, "specialty" colors, because these colors take some extra engineering. It may be a matter of creating not one stack of oxides, but two or more, so that not just one color is being reflected, but a number of colors which combine to create that particularly unique color the artist has requested. This means at least twice the time is required to create the coating because each specialty coating is thicker. For a double stack color, 30 layers may need to be deposited, instead of 15. And of course, if an artist requests that special emerald green reflector, then they won't have any say in the transmitted color. You can control one, but not both. This is why the premium colors of one company are routinely put on black glass rather than clear. The reason being, of course, that if a coating is on black glass, there is no transmission color to be concerned with.

To get green as the transmitted color is even more complicated. Remember that the reflected rainbow is violet/blue/green/yellow/red, but the transmitted rainbow is yellow/magenta/blue/cyan. Green is definitely not one of the naturally transmitted colors created by the basic line of dichroic coatings. So, in order to create a green transmitter, you have to create a stack that reflects blue (yellow transmitter), and another that reflects red (cyan transmitter). *(See figure 5)* Combine those two stacks, and you have a yellow/blue on top of a cyan/red, which results in a green transmitted color. And that dichroic glass sheet will be more expensive, because again, you're using twice as many layers.

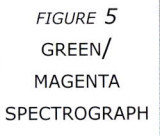

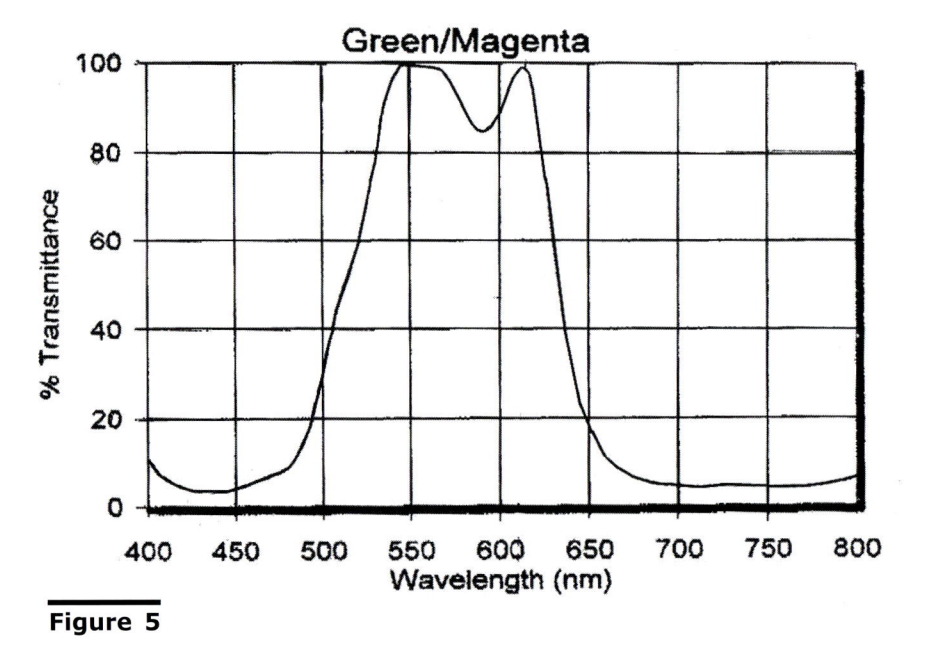

FIGURE 5
GREEN/
MAGENTA
SPECTROGRAPH

Figure 5

What all this information means to the glass artist, is that there is predictability with regard to the transmitted versus reflected colors of dichroic glass. And this predictability applies to hot glass as well as flat glass applications, though the physics are a bit different. But we'll address fusing dichroic glass and the affects of heat on the coatings a little later.

Chapter 2

Terminology Confusion

Defining a Common Language

The language of interference filter and vacuum deposition technology already exists. Rooted in the science of physics, it is an exact language. Unfortunately, the first companies manufacturing dichroic coatings for glass art had to create all new definitions for listing colors, coding glass, and even describing the post-firing color shifts. The results remain a confusion of terms with overlapping yet disparate definitions.

Premium

Nearly every dichroic coating manufacturer has its premium line, but it's important to realize that the term is non-specific; what the term signifies varies from company to company. Both Austin Thin Films and Coatings By Sandberg use the term Premium to describe a group of transmitted colors, such as green, red, silver, orange or teal, which originate outside the standard reflected rainbow. Because these transmitted colors require time and more than one stack during production, the coatings are thicker and more expensive.

Colors

As already mentioned, each manufacturer has its own method of naming colors. One manufacturer may make a distinction between "yellow" and "gold", or "violet" and "purple", another may not. One manufacturer uses "teal" to describe blue-green, another uses "turquoise" to describe the same shade. "Copper," "dark red," "rust," "orange," and "salmon," may all refer to very similar shades of red. And, just to complicate already complicated matters, if the dichroic coating is on clear glass, you will have both the transmitted color and reflected color listed, even when the transmitted color may be almost non-existent. This is the case with the CBS red/silver-blue. There is such an intense reflected silver-blue, that there is barely any energy left for the transmitted red.

It's also worth noting that when a dichroic manufacturer lists a color as "rainbow", you could be getting almost any variation of the reflected rainbow, with any of the available colors as the center color. Remember that the only difference between the dichroic coating process which produces a rainbow and the process which produces a single color is the rotation of the glass during coating. Rotation creates a uniform coating; glass that is stationary results in a rainbow coating. One company has developed a rainbow with light blue at the center, changing to blue, violet, and yellow at the edges. Another manufacturer has blue/violet at the center, with dark red at the edges. The proportion of each color of the spectrum apparent on a sheet of rainbow glass may vary, as may the intensity, hue and saturation of the colors.

Photo 5

As an example, I purchased a sheet of rainbow, thin rolled, smooth dichroic on black to use in my stenciling work. Imagine my dismay when I received the sheet and nearly a third of the rainbow consisted of blue/violet. Since I was going to be fusing this glass, I knew that this whole area would shift beyond the visible violet spectrum and was, therefore, unusable for my application. At nearly $1 per square inch, it was a costly lesson.

How could I have avoided paying for so much dichroic that I couldn't use? What I've learned to do since then, is to communicate with the distributor. When I call with my order I will explain how I plan on using the glass, and this lets the distributor or manufacturer know exactly which part of the rainbow I need to avoid. Adding this extra step in the ordering process has worked well for me, and I haven't had a similar occurrence since.

PATTERNS

At first glance it would seem that describing the process of making patterned dichroic glass would be a simple thing. A stencil of some repeating pattern is put in the way of the deposition. It blocks the traveling metallic oxide vapors from attaching to the substrate glass and, voila! Patterns on the glass. Well, it's not quite that simple.

If the stencil completely blocks the coating (as is the intention), the thickness of the stack goes from 100% down to zero. And, anytime a dichroic coating changes thickness, it changes color. The result is that patterned glass generally produces rainbow colors; a thickness going from 100% to zero forces the coating down through the reflected rainbow. This is the reason that there are no specific color options when the patterns are listed in the various manufacturers' catalogs. Every manufacturer has its own selection of patterns. Each also has the ability to produce specialty patterns based on custom orders from individual glass artists.

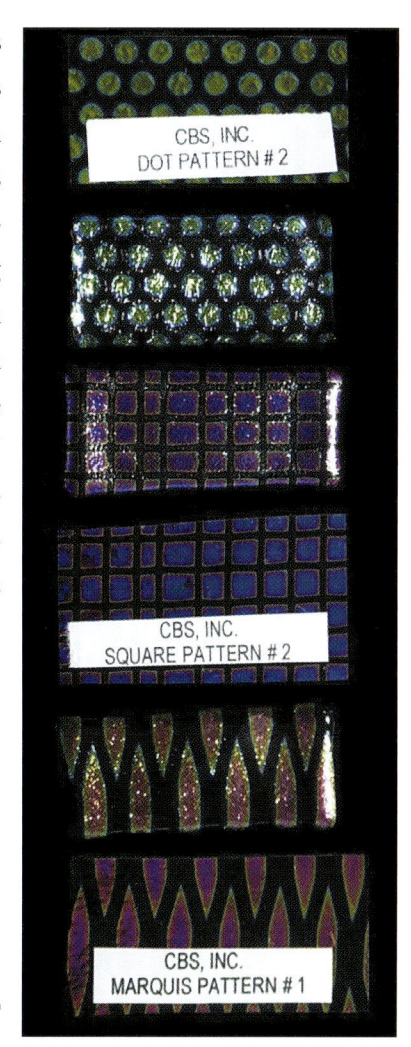

Photo 6

PHOTO 6
VARIOUS PATTERNED DICHROIC GLASS

CODING

Austin Thin Films uses the substrate glass source in its code; e.g., UTG-PI (Uroboros thin granite, pink/turquoise). Coatings By Sandberg doesn't use the substrate source, but lists both the transmitted and reflected color in its code; i.e., P/T (pink/teal). A distributor that buys dichroic glass from a manufacturer and sells it to the glass artist may, for inventory purposes, add their own codes to the manufacturers'. In addition to coding the dichroic colors, manufacturers or distributors may add coding for the substrate glass, thickness, texture, and/or pattern. One company has even coded the "third" color, the shift color which appears when a piece of dichroic glass is tilted at a 45-degree angle.

FOR A CHART OF COMPARATIVE CODINGS, SEE APPENDIX B

The difficulty with naming this shift color is that it changes with the degree of angle at which it is viewed. For example, a cyan/copper sheet (cyan transmitted, copper reflected) will appear golden when held at an angle. But if you increase the angle, to look at the glass even more steeply, the color will continue to lighten to an almost yellow-green. This adds to the confusion that already exists in identifying colors.

What must be remembered is that there will always be a predictable relationship between the reflected and transmitted color, but there's no substitute for actually seeing the glass. Even though each manufacturer works with the same laws of physics and the same technology base, there will continue to be variances in color distinction, uniformity and nomenclature.

There are several terms that are exact and consistent among manufacturers. Their definitions (as they relate to dichroic glass) are the same across the board.

TRANSMISSION

Refers to the passage of light through the glass. The transmitted color is typically the first color listed when coding dichroic coatings on clear glass. The transmission rainbow is yellow, magenta, cyan and blue.

REFLECTION

Refers to the light that strikes the glass and is reflected off. The reflected color is the only one listed when a dichroic coating is on black or other opaque glass. The reflected rainbow is violet/blue, green, yellow and red.

COLOR SHIFT

Refers to the directional change in reflected color when dichroic glass is held at a 45-degree angle from the primary reflected color. Also refers to the color resulting when dichroic glass is heated. In dichroic art glass, the direction of the shifted reflected color would always be down, or, toward the blue/violet end of the spectrum. Additionally, the transmitted color would likewise shift down from blue toward the yellow.

SOME TIPS TO MINIMIZE CONFUSION

· If possible, buy a sample set of the available dichroic colors. If you intend to fuse the glass, familiarize yourself with the various manufacturers of dichroic coatings. Ask questions of your distributors; find out which manufacturers they use.

· Ask for catalogs and keep them handy when ordering.

· When buying dichroic glass, copy the code from the wrapper (if provided) and tape it to a small sample of the glass for reference.

—or—

· When buying for fusing, cut the samples in half, mark each, and fuse one half for pre- and post-firing comparison.

Chapter 3

Adding Heat to Dichroic Glass

I am sure that the first time a glass artist heated dichroic glass, intentionally or not, there was a gasp of surprise at the result. We know for a fact that the manufacturers of technical dichroic coatings had little or no concern for the affects of high heat on their coatings. However, when glass artists began torchworking and kiln-fusing dichroic coatings, it quickly became apparent that a whole new set of problems needed to be addressed.

Heating dichroic glass affects the coatings on so many levels that each will be addressed individually, before being discussed in overall terms.

PHOTO 7
PRE-FUSED GLASS AND POST-FUSED COLOR SHIFT

Photo 7

THE COLOR SHIFT

When the dichroic coating is laid down, it creates an extraordinarily thin crystal structure, approximately 3 to 5 millionths of an inch thick. When you heat that structure, the crystals begin to reorient, and the layer becomes denser, but at the same time, thinner. Something akin to the way glass itself anneals. And, as we've learned, the thickness of the layer determines color.

23

Therefore, as the coating thins (approximately 7%), the color shifts down toward the blue/violet. For example, green-gold shifts to teal, blue shifts to violet, copper shifts to gold, etc. What is essential for the glass artist to realize and remember, is that this heat-related color shift is itself affected by a number of things: the temperature, the length of time at that temperature, and the number of times the glass is heated. The first, major shift is fairly predictable but, if you're firing a bowl 3 times during its creation, the dichroic color will continue to shift a little bit more each time. What does that mean to the hot glass artist? It means that when the artist is creating a design and conceptualizing a finished product using dichroic coatings, the post-firing color must be planned for, and the pre-firing color must be selected with a knowledge of what will happen to the coating over the length of time and temperature the glass will be exposed to the heat of the kiln, torch, or furnace.

CRAZING

This is the term typically applied to the "cracking" that occurs when some dichroic coatings are heated. It can range from something as minimal as fine, but distinct cracks in a small area of dichroic coating, all the way up to radically disturbed areas that resemble a parched desert ground, or the webbing of a lava field as it cools. Whether this effect is going to be intentionally created or carefully avoided, an understanding of its cause is necessary for the hot glass artist.

Like everything else in the universe, dichroic coatings have a rate of thermal expansion. Those of us who work in warm and hot glass know that thermal expansion describes the amount and rate at which any given substance expands or contracts at a particular temperature. Warm and hot glass artists use the coefficient of thermal expansion to determine the compatibility of the glass(es) that they use in fusing. If two or more pieces of glass with significantly different co-efficients of expansion (COE) are fused together, the stresses created by their incompatibility upon cooling will cause fracturing in the glass.

Dichroic coatings are not compatible with glass. That statement bears repeating. The dichroic coating is not compatible with the glass substrate to which it is attached. Therefore, when you heat dichroic-coated glass, there will be some level of incompatibility. As the glass expands and contracts, the coating expands and contracts at a different rate. Whether you see the result of that incompatibility or not depends on a host of circumstances. Thickness of the coating has a definite effect on whether the coating will "craze." *"Thickness" here does not refer to the stack of oxides that, together, produces color, but the physical number of layers of the coating that are placed on the glass by the manufacturer.*

When any dichroic coating is heated, depending again on temperature and length of time at temperature, it will craze and break into tiny platelets. If the crystal structure is highly stressed (a quality-related function) the resultant pieces will be much finer and smaller. If the structure is more relaxed and thermally compatible (with itself and the glass), the pieces will be larger and more stable. The degree of crazing and distortion of the coating will vary from run to run (a run is considered to be a controlled number of coated glass sheets created at the same time in the same batch), and from manufacturer to manufacturer.

During heating, the difference in thermal expansion between the coating and glass will become more pronounced, and the dichroic will begin to curl. The crazed pieces will no longer be flat. They will become any number of small, curved shapes scattering more light back at you. That's why fired dichroic glass has the appearance it does. It's brighter (kicking more energy back) because now the pieces of coating are actually curved; the end result is a non-compatible inclusion floating around in the piece of glass. If you see a dichroic coating that has been stretched way out by a glass blower, you will be able to see the small platelets of color. However, as long as the individual "stacks" are intact, you will continue to have color. The layers, though in pieces, have maintained their crystal integrity. If, for any reason, that integrity is disturbed, you will lose or change the color irretrievably.

Photo 8

PHOTO 8 DISTORTED, FUSED DICHROIC PATTERN IN GLASS

Another, less technical reason for crazing is viscosity. The dichroic coating is a crystal structure, as mentioned previously. Some of its properties include expansion and contraction, but the temperature at which the glass substrate becomes too viscous to maintain its own integrity is far lower than the temperature at which the dichroic coating will melt. The substrate glass will soften and begin to change shape, while the crystal structure of the dichroic coating remains unchanged. The result is a craze, or cracking of the coating as the more viscous glass moves beneath it.

Which brings us to another myth: you can't fuse two pieces of dichroic glass together, coating to coating. Well, it's not really a myth, but a common misconception. Technically, the statement is correct, in that the temperature has to be upwards of 3000 degrees to actually melt the crystal structure of the dichroic coatings together. If you've ever placed a piece of dichroic glass coating side up, and inadvertently fused another piece of dichroic on top with the coating side down, you'll have noticed that the top piece doesn't melt into the bottom piece at all. Instead, it shrinks up into a domed bubble, which eventually may pop off.

Knowing and understanding the incompatibility relationship between the substrate and the coating may permit the glass artist to create some very interesting effects by fusing dichroic glass coating to coating (with a little help). In Chapter Four you will see such a method.

PHOTO 9
BURNOUT ON KILN GLASS

Photo 9

BURNOUT

This may be the most vexing, yet misunderstood problem that has affected hot glass artists using dichroic glass. And probably the most easily avoided.

It had always been my understanding that burnout was a result of temperature only. The dichroic coating simply got too hot and burned off the glass, leaving behind a gray, muddy mess. I'm sure I'm not the only hot glass artist who has avoided putting the coating directly into a torch flame, or taken painstaking precautions to always cover the dichroic with clear glass before full fusing. But in reality, burnout happens as a result of a much more complex set of circumstances. This information is essential to the torch-working and furnace-working glass artist, but will serve to help every glass artist to understand the fundamentals of burnout.

The key to understanding burnout is the fact that the dichroic coating is comprised of stacks of low refractive and high refractive index materials. The low refractive index material, for the most part, is quartz crystal. The high refractive index materials used in developing a filter stack include titanium, zirconium, and others. These are the oxides which, when in a vapor state, attach to the substrate to create the crystal structure that becomes the dichroic coating. Each of these metal oxides has different inherent physical characteristics, and each must be attached to the substrate in a manner that ensures that they remain clear. The one thing that all of these metal oxides have in common is that they only maintain their integrity in an oxide state. For those of us without a degree in chemistry this means that each oxide contains oxygen molecules which must remain a component of that crystalline structure. If you take this dichroic crystal layer and begin removing the oxygen from its structure, or force it into a sub-oxide state, the molecular composition of the dichroic coating changes, and it will become brown, gray, or otherwise change color.

In the early days of dichroic art glass, there were far more inconsistencies in the manufacture of the coatings. The kinds of metallic oxides used were inferior to those used today. The affect of heat on those oxides was not well understood, and burnout was a common occurrence. As techniques improved, and the use of metallic oxides became more sophisticated, the reasons for burnout became better understood. And, as the number of dichroic glass manufacturers increased and competition for the narrow market of glass artists increased, controlling burnout at working temperatures for those artists became a major focus.

We now know that in order for dichroic coatings to maintain their integrity and crystal structure, they must remain in an oxygen environment. The first clue came from beadmakers who complained about burnout. The situations were all such that they were using bottled gas or torches which could not control the flame's oxygen content. As these torchworkers cranked up the gas to create more heat, they created a greater reducing flame. When the dichroic coatings were placed in these reducing flames, oxygen molecules began to leave the surface of the coatings, destroying the crystal structure. The result was a gray mess where beautiful color had been. So it was discovered, after much empirical data was collected, that burnout was related as much to structure as to the thickness of the coating. And anything that alters or compromises the structure of the dichroic coating will increase the chances of burnout.

As a hot glass artist, you may find that you have incidents of burnout that turn out to be sheet-specific. If one part of a sheet of dichroic glass is susceptible to burnout, the rest of that same sheet may very well experience the same problem. In addition, because burnout is related to structure, there are other manufacturing variables which may affect a coating's propensity for burnout. The rates of deposition, the pressure of the deposition, and the temperature of the substrate at the time of deposition, are all factors that might increase the risk of burnout.

With this understanding, the hot glass artist working with dichroic glass in the torch or furnace can certainly decrease the chances of burnout by maintaining as much of an oxidizing flame as possible. If working with reducing lusters or similar inclusions that require a reducing flame, the artist can either avoid working concurrently with dichroic coatings, or make certain that the coatings are well protected, most commonly with a coating of clear glass. And, as always, be knowledgeable about the source of your dichroic coatings, and keep records of any problems that arise in firing. The glass artist may well be able to detect important patterns in procedure or glass origins that can be corrected so that future occurrences of the problem are reduced or eliminated.

I'd like to make some general comments regarding heat and dichroic coatings. There are certain conclusions that can be drawn based on research and the results of observation. Although the physics behind interference filters and vacuum deposition is well known, each manufacturer has its own method(s) of tweaking the formula. Much like four bakers who all have the same basic recipe for chocolate cake, yet each will bake a cake that tastes a bit different, has a different consistency, and looks quite individual. Take two sheets of copper reflector on black, thin-rolled Bullseye, COE 90 dichroic glass from two different coating manufacturers. You might reasonably expect that if one piece was cut from the same place on each sheet, and exposed to a fusing temperature in the same kiln for the same length of time, the results would be the same. Unfortunately the hot glass artist could very well find to his or her dismay that one piece has shifted to gold, while the other has shifted all the way to green/gold. One piece may be extraordinarily shiny in sunlight, while the other is more subdued. One piece may even have some visible gray burnout, while the other is clean.

If there is one consistency involved in fusing dichroic glass, it's the fact that there still exists quite a bit of inconsistency. Only direct experimentation and observation will tell the hot glass artist which dichroic glass provides the most satisfactory result for each particular application. It may be reassuring to know that dichroic coating manufacturers continue to refine and perfect the process to better meet our expectations of quality, consistency and uniformity.

Chapter 4

The Techniques of Using Dichroics in Glass Art

The purpose of this chapter is to offer some basic information on using dichroic glass in general applications. Some of the techniques and tips may seem academic, some trivial or even ridiculously obvious, but all of this information is part of the solid foundation necessary to begin working successfully with dichroic art glass.

GLASS PREPARATION

Whether the plan is to use dichroic coatings in flat glass work or hot glass work, there are certain techniques to remember when cutting the glass. First, due to their thinness, dichroic coatings are highly susceptible to scratches, especially when not fused. That means dichroic glass should be stored carefully, and stacking pieces or scraping pieces against each other should be avoided. In addition, when cutting dichroic glass, the artist should attempt to cut on the non-coated side whenever possible. This may require attaching or tracing pattern pieces backwards. This will be a moot point when cutting highly textured dichroic glass, since the coating is almost always placed on the textured side. If you do use a glass cutter on the dichroic coating, however, you will notice a definite chipping on the edges.

PHOTO 10
CHIPPED DICHROIC EDGES ON A GROUND GLASS PIECE.

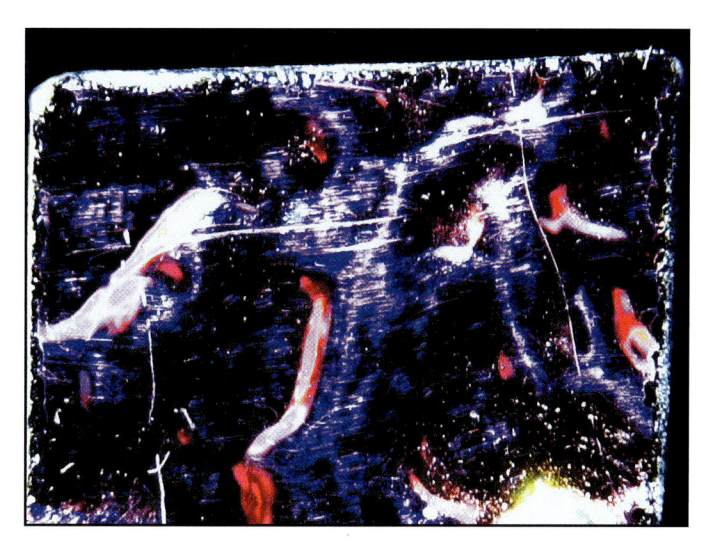

Photo 10

Similarly, when grinding dichroic glass, it is recommended that you grind the pieces upside-down if possible, as this minimizes the incidence of chipping caused by the grinding head. Even if most of the chipping on the edges will ultimately be covered by lead came or foil in flat glass applications, the goal is to keep the coating as intact as possible. You will also notice that the direction in which you move the pieces against the spinning, grinding head will affect the degree of chipping that occurs at the edges of the coating.

When chipping occurs prior to fusing, remember that the coating will shrink to varying degrees, and you may find that what was barely seen at the outer edge of your piece becomes quite prominent post-firing. This will be especially true if fusing your piece with a protective coating of clear glass.

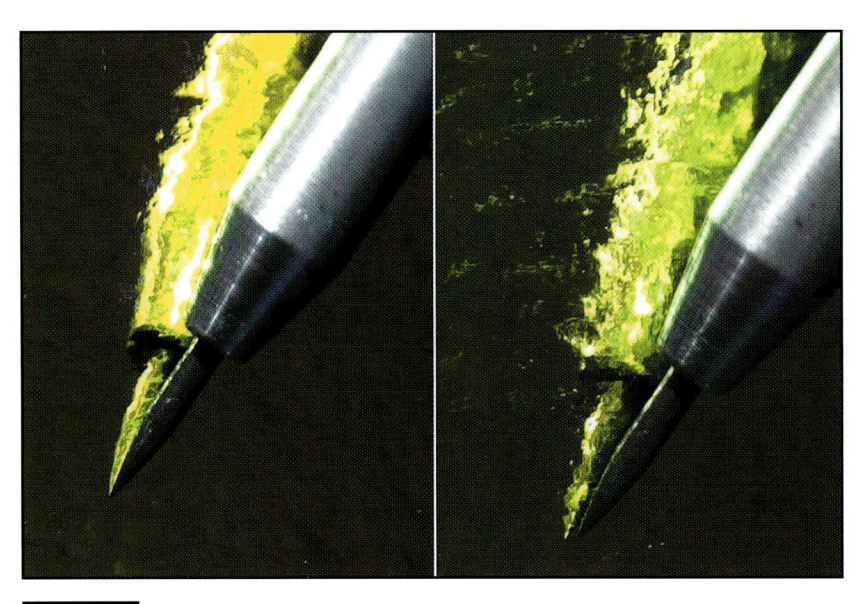

Photo 11

PHOTO 11
METHOD OF DETERMINING WHICH SIDE OF THE GLASS IS COATED.
LEFT: COATED SIDE UP
RIGHT: COATED SIDE DOWN.

The question most often asked by my students is probably, "When using dichroic coatings on smooth, clear glass, how do you tell which side is coated?" I use a technique that I've never found to fail, and it's simple: take your piece of dichroic glass in one hand and a pointed object in the other. It could be a toothpick or pointed pencil. I use a metal compass tip. Now, hold your piece of dichroic glass (pick a side, any side) at an angle, and gradually lower your point toward it until you can see its reflection in the dichroic glass. You may have to adjust the angle of the dichroic and/or point to get the best reflection. Bring the two together so that the tip of the point finally touches the dichroic glass. Look carefully. Can you see the reflection of the point on the dichroic? Does the point actually appear to be touching the glass without a space in between? Or, does there seem to be a gap between the point and the dichroic glass? If the reflection of the point appears to actually meet the point, you have the dichroic coating side up. If there appears to be a gap between the surface of the dichroic and the pointed object, then the dichroic coating is on the bottom, away from the point. Why?

If you have the dichroic side down, you are seeing the reflection of the compass tip through the layer of clear glass, resulting in the appearance of a gap between the two. It may take a bit of practice, but this is a no-fail method. Ultimately, even this technique will become unnecessary, as you will be able to tell whether you're looking at the dichroic coating up or down by the appearance of depth within the glass. I've had students actually admit that they'd never used clear, smooth dichroic glass because it was too frustrating trying to distinguish between the sides. Just remember that it's far more aggravating to guess, only to find out after firing that you were wrong and the piece is ruined.

FLAT GLASS APPLICATIONS

The very first uses of dichroic glass involved taking bits and pieces from broken and abandoned coated bulbs and filters, drilling holes in them, and selling them as craft jewelry. This is still a basic use of the glass. If the sharp edges are ground for safety, dichroic glass can be glued using epoxy, UV glass glues, or the cyanoacrylate glues. Since the transmitted colors are cumulative (blue transmitter on top of yellow transmitter will appear as green), layering can create interesting effects. The one caution, as mentioned previously, is the vulnerability of the unfused coating to scratches. If the coating is on clear glass, the obvious solution is to put the top piece, coated side down.

The decision to use dichroic glass as part of a copper foiled or leaded piece can be made for any number of reasons. It can add variety and vitality. It can add dimension. And its color-shifting ability is the perfect way to impart dynamic motion to an otherwise static piece.

In Peter McGrain's panel, "Good Exposure," the overall work is the result of 3 distinct panels, foiled and soldered together. Peter had OCLI coat float glass with multiple

Photo 12

Photo 13

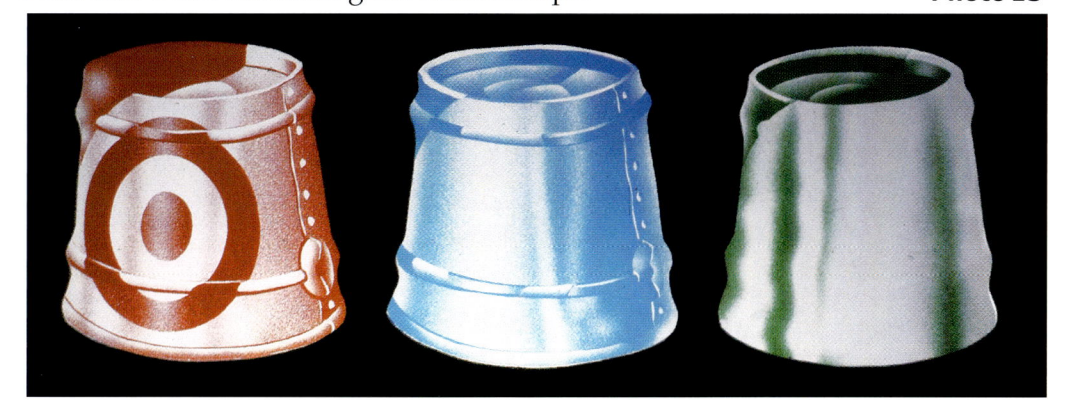

PHOTO 12
PETER MCGRAIN'S "GOOD EXPOSURE."

PHOTO 13
DETAIL: "GOOD EXPOSURE." THE THIN COATING ALLOWED FOR DELICATE CONTROL DURING REMOVAL WITH THE BLASTER, RESULTING IN EXTREMELY TIGHT DETAIL. IN MOST AREAS OF THE PANEL THE VISUAL EFFECT IS ACCOMPLISHED BY LAYERING THREE LAYERS OF THE MATERIAL, AS IN THE BREAKDOWN OF THE BUCKET SECTION.

31

Dichroics

PHOTO 14:
RAMSES AND
CHARIOT

layers of dichroic coatings. He then used a sandblast chamber to remove various areas of the layers in different ways. Then, by layering the glass, he created an incredible 3-D effect.

Photo 14

Once fused, dichroic glass can enhance flat glasswork by providing texture and a level of complexity and detail otherwise impossible in lead came or foiled glass work alone. Pieces that are too small to foil can be fused together and designs, which would be diminished by the presence of lead or solder lines, can be fused first and then added to the piece. In this photo, the insert shows more clearly the detail in the figure. The glass in the Pharaoh's headpiece is made of small pieces of dichroic glass fused on a larger piece of dichroic reeded glass. His eyes (and that of the horse) are fused for a 3-dimensional look. His arm and neck jewelry are dichroic clear, unfused glass. The overall size of this work was 3 ft x 2 ft and contained over 350 individually foiled and soldered pieces.

Fusing together layers of dichroic glass can create colors and effects impossible with traditional, colored glass.

There is a certain danger, however, in using dichroic glass to enhance flat glasswork. When first working with dichroic glass, the tendency is to overuse it. It looks incredible, is immediately eye-catching, and adds great appeal and marketability. However, it is possible to overdo the use of dichroic glass in the execution of a piece, just as it is possible to overdo the use of any color or texture of traditional colored glass. The majority of glass artists experienced in working with dichroics will agree that, in most instances, dichroic glass is at its best when it is used least. As an embellishment, a focal point, or to break the monotony, it is unrivaled. Overused, dichroic can make an otherwise well designed piece appear garish, gaudy, ostentatious or pretentious. Of course, if over-the-top is what you want, then go for it. Just remember that, at about $1 per square inch, the final cost of adding substantial amounts of dichroic glass to the piece may price it out of the range of your target customer.

So, when is enough, enough? Experience will temper exuberance with common sense. Ultimately, it's a matter of personal preference, but knowing there is in fact a line to be drawn will help the glass artist to find their own and keep it in sight.

Architectural Applications

There is an increasing demand for dichroic coatings on glass for inclusion in architectural structures. One of the first major applications of dichroic glass as structure was Peter McGrain's 1996 commission for the Rochester Airport. Various manufacturers of dichroic coatings have told me that since the installation of that commission, they've seen an astounding increase in orders for dichroic coatings to be placed on various types of glass blocks, tiles, etc. For those structures needing to withstand the climate, the final, low index coating (usually quartz) is increased to afford added protection.

PHOTO 15 PETER MCGRAIN'S "MONUMENT" 25' x 100'. DENNIS SCHMIDT, THEN OF TLC, COATED THE GLASS SPECIFICALLY FOR THIS APPLICATION. OVER 200 TWENTY-ONE INCH CIRCULAR SHEETS OF DICHROIC GLASS WERE USED IN THE PIECE.

Photo 15

PHOTO 16
DIFFERENT SHAPES OF DICHROIC GLASS SHEETS.

WARM AND HOT GLASS

Using dichroic coatings in hot glass applications is an entirely different ball of wax, so-to-speak. As long as your substrate glasses are compatible, dichroic glass can be fused right along with uncoated compatible glass. As I explained earlier, there are currently two major types of dichroic glasses available to the hot glass artist. Dichroic coating on clear, and dichroic coating on black. This is not to say that you couldn't have the dichroic coating of your choice placed on other colors. For the most part, any dichroic coating manufacturer will take a special order and coat any color, texture, and/or thickness you could want. Manufacturers Bullseye, Uroboros, and Spectrum, all stock glasses tested compatible for fusing and available with dichroic coatings. Float glass, Moretti, and even borosilicate glass (Pyrex®) with dichroic coatings may be obtained from certain distributors or manufacturers directly, often without placing a special order.

However, the reality of the situation is that the vast majority of dichroic coatings currently available come on either clear or black glass. The most common is thin-rolled, though full-thickness (1/8") sheets are also readily available. Full sized sheets vary in size, from 16" square, to 19" circles, or 19" pumpkins (top and bottom cut off). The size and shape are determined by the configuration of the vacuum chamber that the manufacturer uses, and by the initial size of the sheet when it comes from the glassmaker. Sheets from certain dichroic coating companies have a "clip" mark, where the glass was held in place in the chamber during coating, and on which no coating is visible. Sheets from other dichroic companies may have been clipped on the corners, but every square inch of purchased glass is coated.

TORCHWORKED GLASS

You can prevent coating burnout by using the oxidizing portion of the flame. If possible increase the oxygen to the flame rather than increasing the fuel to create a hotter flame. Avoid using reducing lusters and unprotected dichroic coatings in the same application. Remember that the cut, raw edges of a piece of dichroic glass will get hottest soonest, and may actually reach 3000 degrees Fahrenheit well before the remainder of the piece, increasing the risk of burnout. Take extra care when adding dichroic black glass to round beads and marbles. It is very easy to begin winding the glass strip with the dichroic coating inward, hiding the color from view. Also, it is very important to remember that the black substrate glass will melt and expand far more than the dichroic coating, and some practice will be needed to control the position and direction of the colors so that they do not become hidden by the black substrate glass.

Photo 17

PHOTO 17
TORCHWORKED BEAD BY LEAH FAIRBANKS

FURNACE-WORKED GLASS

The information needed to use dichroic coatings successfully in the furnace is similar to the torchworking information. Try to maintain your hot gather in the most oxygen-rich part of the furnace during and after adding your dichroic glass. If working with large amounts of clear glass, such as paperweights and tableware, be aware that if the coating is allowed to stretch and break, bits of the coating may come loose and become floating inclusions in the glass. Also, the higher internal temperature of a large gather can make it difficult to prevent the shape of the captured dichroic from distorting and/or shrinking. However, being able to layer dichroic coated clear glass over other layers of dichroic coatings gives the glass artist using a furnace more flexibility in color design and effects.

Photo 18

PHOTO 18
FIRE OPAL WORLD BY REBECCA STEWART

Chapter 4

35

Tips and Techniques

Fused Dichroic Coatings on Clear Vs. on Black

The reasons for choosing one over the other may seem obvious, but they're worth mentioning for those readers who may be totally unfamiliar with dichroic coatings. There is nothing as dramatic as taking a piece of fused, clear, dichroic glass and moving it from a white to a dark background. The transmitted colors change to the reflected colors, and inevitably, "oohs" and "aahs" are elicited from viewers. When planning the design, however, one thing needs to be remembered: you can see through clear dichroic! If you are making a piece of jewelry—a brooch or pendant— it would be wise to consider the setting before committing to the glass. A pin finding glued to the back of a clear dichroic cabochon will be clearly visible through the glass. The same goes for any setting. Unless you're planning on putting a bezel around the edge, or drilling a hole for a jump-ring, you might want to consider something other than clear.

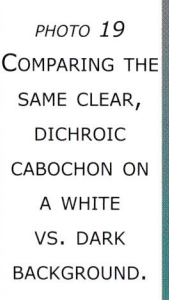

PHOTO 19
COMPARING THE SAME CLEAR, DICHROIC CABOCHON ON A WHITE VS. DARK BACKGROUND.

Photo 19

On the other hand, fused dichroic coatings on black glass have the disadvantage of having no transmitted color at all. Depending on the total area of dichroic, you may be able to see a pronounced color shift upon angling the piece, but there will be no dramatic transmitted-to-reflected color change. Although, there are other benefits to the use of dichroic on black glass, and when used in conjunction with dichroic on clear, some spectacular effects can be achieved.

Layering dichroic glass

Previously we discussed the light spectrum, and the basic colors of the dichroic rainbow. It is interesting to note that combining transmitted colors, i.e., layering one atop the other, results in a new color that follows the traditional artist's color wheel. For example: a yellow-transmitted piece of dichroic fused on top of a cyan-transmitted piece will result in a green-transmitted piece (yellow plus cyan equals green). However, if you take yellow-transmitted dichroic glass and fuse it on top of a cyan on a black piece (which means there is no transmitted light), the yellow-transmitted color will no longer be evident. That's because the black glass prevents any transmission of light and only the reflected color of the coating is visible over the cyan base glass. But you will see the result of layered reflected colors. I often use a cyan-reflected coating on clear over deep oranges and/or yellows and greens for an ethereal, ghostly effect.

Which brings us to the use of plain, uncoated clear glass over dichroic coatings. The appearance of unprotected dichroic glass after fusing is totally different from the look you get when you fuse clear glass on top of the coating. Depending on the original finish of the unprotected dichroic surface, there may be a shiny, vaguely metallic, or crystalline look after firing. The reflective energy will be intense and will appear directly on the surface of the glass. If, however, you place a piece of clear glass over the dichroic coating and then fire it, several incredible things happen. First, any texture present will be flattened, but will retain more of its integrity. Next, the colors may shift to a lesser degree than any unprotected coating around the coated area. Lastly, there will be a wonderful illusion of depth, as though you are seeing the coated glass across a perceptible distance. This last effect is a result of the clear glass acting as a lens, slowing the light that enters.

The most important reason for choosing to use the technique of placing clear glass on top of dichroic coatings is to protect them. However durable they may appear after firing, the thickness of the coatings is measured in microns. A clear glass cap will help avoid potential nicks and scratches, and increase the overall durability of the piece.

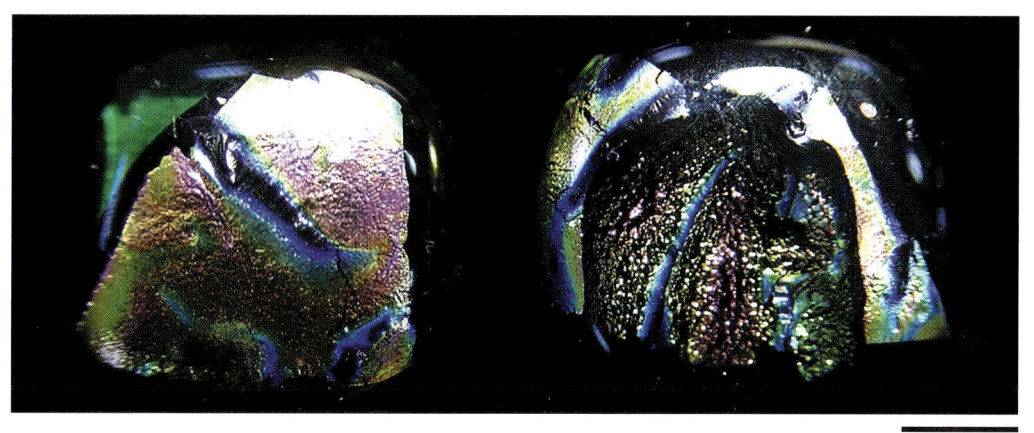

Photo 20

PHOTO 20 FIRED DICHROIC WITH AND WITHOUT CLEAR GLASS CAP.

Chapter 4

SPECIAL EFFECTS AND DICHROIC COATINGS

STENCILING

I had been stenciling designs on clear glass using a commercial acid cream for a number of years before seeing my first piece of dichroic-on-black glass. Immediately, I realized the dramatic effects that could be achieved by contrasting the intense colors of the coating with the underlying black substrate. At first, I used traditional methods in creating my stencils. I transferred a design onto a resist film using carbon paper, placed the film on the glass and then cut out the unwanted pieces with an X-ACTO® knife. I discovered quickly, however, that cutting out the film on the glass meant potential disaster for the thin, dichroic coating. In addition, the small size and minute detail of the designs I was using made using the frisket film nearly impossible and very time-consuming. Shellie Carder, then my wire-sculpting mentor, laughed when she heard how much time I was spending in stencil-cutting, and gave me a quick and easy solution.

She handed me a permanent marker. Yep, you're reading it right, a black, fine-tipped marker! There have been other neat, little items I've learned to use since, but that black marker changed the way I was able to create designs. It allowed me to get to a level of detail I would have never been able to achieve if I'd continued to cut itsy-bitsy pieces out of plastic film.

Simply put, you use the marker as a resist. There are variances among the different brands of markers, and I won't be more specific here for fear of giving the appearance of preferring one brand to the other. Suffice to say you need to experiment until you find the one that works the best for your particular application.

The trick to using a permanent marker as a resist is that you have to be very careful to fully cover the area you don't want removed. This is working in reverse. What you draw will remain, the acid cream will remove everything else left untouched. After you draw your design, let it dry completely, then go over it again. There are several brands of etching cream, all of which will get the job done. Pick the one you find works the best for you. If you haven't used acid cream before, make sure you read the label carefully, including all of the precautions. Wear protective eye and hand gear, and use a disposable brush to apply the cream. Most importantly, apply the cream in the vicinity of a source of running water. Unlike a typical etching cream application where you can allow the cream to remain on the glass for several minutes, you'll find that if you don't keep very careful track of time, in seconds, the cream will eat through both the resist marker and the dichroic coating, leaving you with a pristine, and very unusable piece of black (or clear) glass.

At this point, you need to remember what we've learned about dichroic coatings. Color is determined by differences in thickness. Granted, we're talking about differences measured in microns, but in this instance, it's enough. Each color of dichroic coating will react to the acid cream at a different rate. Two pieces of dichroic from the same sheet will take the same time to etch, but the same color from two different sheets may react differently in a matter of seconds. Theoretically, the violets and blues will take less time to etch than the reds and oranges. Of course, the etch time is also dependent on the manufacturer and the quality of the coating. The bottom line is that you can't treat every color and every piece of dichroic glass the same. After a while you will get a sense of how long to wait, and what to expect. Pick a scrap area of each sheet to experiment with. Eventually this will take you only seconds once you get into the habit.

From the moment the etching cream hits the dichroic coating, it begins eating it away. It will take anywhere from a few seconds up to a minute or two to eat through the coating to the black beneath. This means that you need to think about how and where you're applying the cream, and how long it will take you to apply it. For example, if you have a 2"x2" piece of dichroic glass with a design markered onto it, and you apply the acid cream from the left side to the right side of the glass, the left edge, where you started, will be ready to wash off before the right edge. Further, if you take 15 or so seconds to actually apply the cream, the left side of the design will be ruined or gone by the time the right is ready. The dichroic coating is that thin, and in this instance, the acid cream is that aggressive.

Photo 21

PHOTO 21
POORLY
AND
UNDER-ETCHED
DESIGN.

The correct way to apply etching cream is to drop it liberally from the center to the outside, taking only a second or two. Hold the glass piece up, between your thumb and forefinger, being careful not to get the cream on your skin (it

Dichroics

1. DRAW THE DESIGN WITH A MARKER.

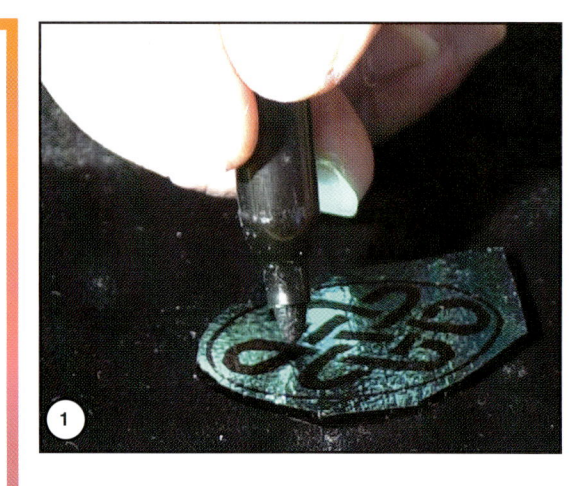

2. REMOVE UNWANTED MARKER WITH TOOTHPICK.

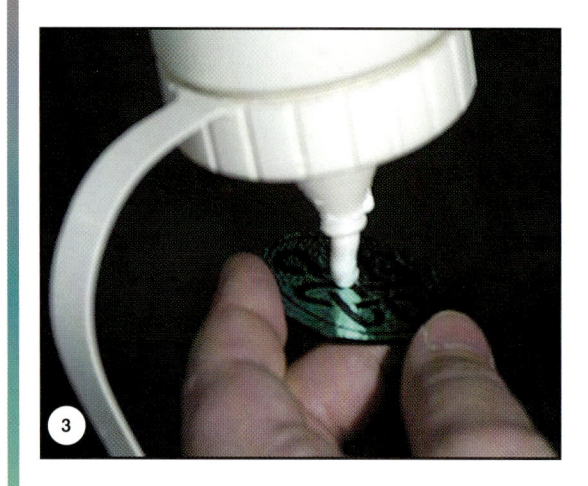

3. ADD ACID CREAM TO CENTER OF PIECE.

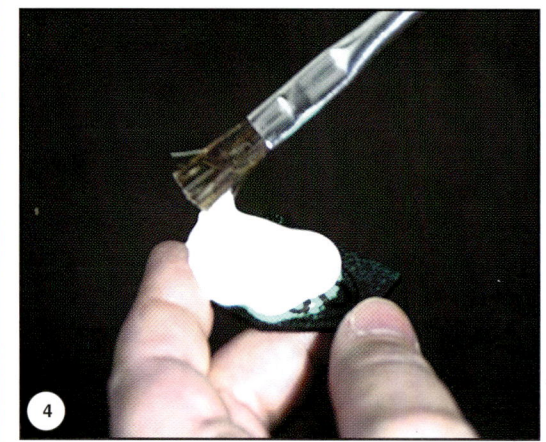

4. SPREAD OUTWARD WITH DISPOSABLE BRUSH.

will irritate, sting or even burn). Select a corner that extends beyond your design as your test corner. Using a dry toothpick, very gently and carefully scrape the etching cream away from the surface of the glass. What you see will depend on exactly how many seconds have elapsed. At the very least, you should see that the shiny, dichroic coating has changed color, dimmed, or may already be almost gone. It's important not to rush. Impatience is your worst enemy. If you wash away the cream too early, it won't have had a chance to remove all the dichroic from the unprotected area, and you will be left with a very nasty, unpleasant ghost of the coating next to the black marker design. If this occurs, the only solution is to reapply the marker, and repeat the process.

Learning how long to wait before you wash the cream off will take the most practice to master. In testing the corner, you need to wait until all of the coating is completely gone from under the cream. Then you need to count to ten (one, one thousand, two, one thousand, etc.). Place the piece under running water and very quickly rinse the remainder of the etching cream from the piece, front and back. Continue to run water over the piece until you are certain all traces of the cream are gone. Then, with the toothpick, rub the marker design under the water. The black ink will begin to come away from the dichroic coating it's been protecting, revealing the (hopefully) intact coating beneath. Dry the piece and, voila! You now have a permanent dichroic design on black, ready to be covered with clear, fusible glass, and fired.

Some tips related to the use of marker on dichroic glass for stenciling:
• Use a dichroic glass with the least

amount of surface texture. The marker will adhere better and reduce design distortion.

• Make sure the glass is very clean before you use the marker. Remove any oils, fingerprints and dirt that could interfere with the ink sticking.

• Once you've completed the design, you can remove any unwanted, stray ink with a moistened toothpick or other round, pointed object (I use a compass point) for shading and highly detailed designs. Test any sharp object you plan to use on a scrap piece of dichroic to be sure it won't scratch the surface.

• When cutting your glass prior to using the marker, plan on leaving an exposed corner to use as a test area after the cream has been applied. Forgetting this step will make it impossible to tell when it's time to wash the cream off without disturbing your design.

• When planning your design, remember that what you mark will remain dichroic glass. All the rest will be removed. If you have a large circle of dichroic glass and fill in a small circle in the center with the marker, you will be left with a small circle of dichroic glass surrounded by solid black glass substrate. That's a very expensive, very small circle, and a whole lot of expensive, dichroic coating washed down the drain. You should, instead, invert the design. Mark over everything but the very small black circle. After etching, you will have a small, black circle surrounded by a large area of dichroic glass. Think ahead.

The importance of covering your finished, stenciled design with clear glass and firing it can't be emphasized enough. Based on what we learned previously about dichroic coatings, you will recall that the melting point of glass is far lower than that of the dichroic coating, which melts at around 3000 degrees

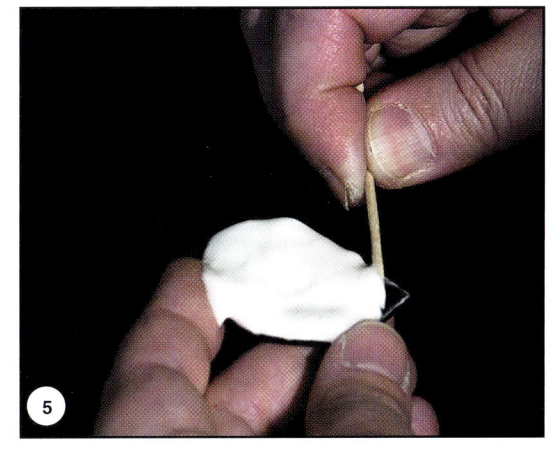

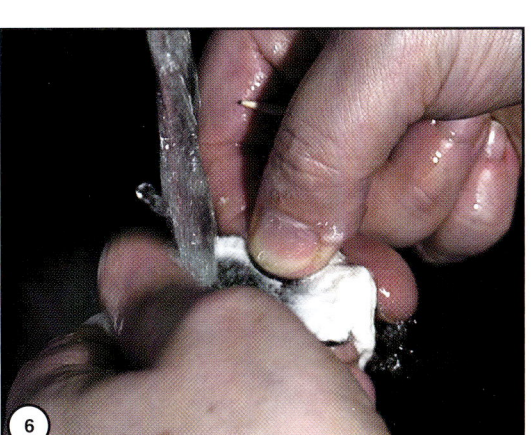

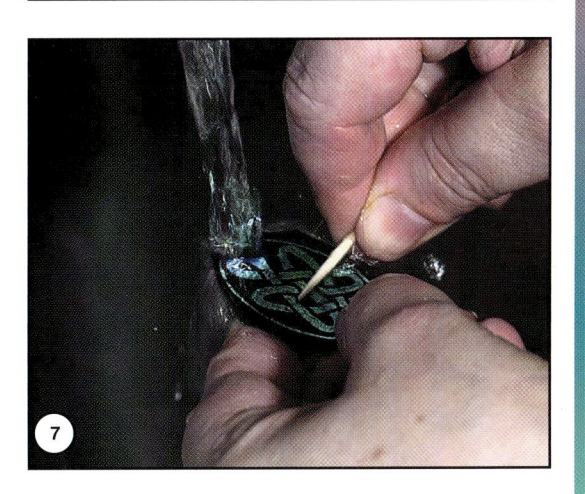

Chapter 4

5. GENTLY PUSH BACK CREAM FROM TEST CORNER.

6. RINSE THOROUGHLY UNDER RUNNING WATER.

7. REMOVE REMAINING MARKER WITH TOOTHPICK.

8. FINISHED DESIGN READY FOR GLASS CAP.

Fahrenheit. Once you have disrupted the integrity of the dichroic coating on a piece of glass you are left with a very thin layer of dichroic coating floating on the glass substrate. If left uncovered and heated to the glass' melting temperature, the crystal structure of the remaining coating will shrink and distort, and the softening glass beneath it will move, pulling and distorting the dichroic even further.

Sandwiching the stenciled design between the substrate and a clear glass cap will not only protect the design; it will capture it between the two pieces of glass. This will prevent distortion to a great degree, and allow the design to appear brighter and clearer when it is viewed through the clear glass. One cautionary note: you must heat the piece just to the point where the edges become round and the surface is shiny, called "fire polishing." Over-firing the piece will allow the softening substrate glass to move more readily, increasing the chances of pulling the dichroic design out of shape and distorting it. Again, proficiency will come with practice.

After you've mastered this process, you might want to consider adding another level of complexity to your designs. Try this: almost immediately after applying the acid cream, experiment by washing the cream off a portion of the design. You'll notice that the shiny appearance of the dichroic coating has disappeared, and the color may even have changed. Allow the remainder of the design to etch to completion and wash off the rest of the etching cream. Remember that color is determined by the thickness of each layer. Try it. You'll be amazed at the variety of effects you can achieve.

There are other methods to stencil dichroic glass. These include using rubber stamps to apply the resist ink, or using a brush to put etching cream directly on the rubber stamp and pressing gently against the glass. Try a commercially made stencil, specifically created for etching, and a dauber to apply the etching cream. These can be found at craft stores and/or stained glass supply stores. Of course, sandblasting dichroic glass will achieve much the same effect, but requires additional equipment, materials and expertise.

INTENTIONAL CRAZING

Under controlled circumstances, crazing in the dichroic surface can look astounding. I sometimes describe it as looking like cooling lava in reverse. There are several ways to achieve this look. I'll mention one briefly, and elaborate more on another.

The first method is simply heating. The blue/violets have thinner layers than the reds so, theoretically, the blue reflected colors craze more easily. However, practical experience shows that the quality and integrity of the glass has more to do with the resulting appearance. The best results are obtained by fusing a coated glass with a clear glass cap. The glass softens; the dichroic coating does not. The coating cracks, and then allows the black substrate glass to show through. If you don't cover some area of dichroic with clear glass before you fuse it, you are much less likely to have any cracking. If you think about it, it makes sense. Without any clear glass on top, the dichroic coating remains intact, and the softening glass beneath it can spread at the edges. However, if you place clear glass on top of the dichroic coating, you will trap the dichroic coating. As the piece heats, both top and bottom glasses soften and begin to move. The trapped coating is stressed by this pulling and given the proper length of time and heat, will split and crack.

There is another method of creating beautiful crazes in the dichroic coating. It is a little more labor intensive, but is also gives much more interesting results. It involves something that has always been considered taboo: placing two dichroic coatings face-to-face.

The typical procedure is to take a piece of dichroic-on-black glass and cover it with another piece of dichroic-on-clear, with the coatings facing each other. Under normal circumstances, this would be an incompatible union since, as we've already learned, the fusing temperature of glass is less than the temperature needed to fuse the dichroic coatings together.

However, if you place at least two additional layers of clear glass on top of the two pieces with coatings facing prior to the initial firing, the weight of the additional glass flowing and moving will almost certainly cause the dichroic coatings to break and crack under the strain. In order to perform this technique successfully, however, two important changes must be made.

First, when stacking the glass, you have to remember that the more pieces you stack, the more the glass will spread when fired. Whether you start with 1/8" standard thickness glass, or thin rolled glass, remember that during fusing, the glass wants to be ¼" thick. If you have four layers of glass, all standard thickness, stacked on top of one another, and the top two are clear, you will have a good deal of clear glass flowing uselessly over the other two pieces onto the kiln shelf. The excess can be clipped or cut away and the resulting piece can then be fire polished. Another method is to make each subsequent layer of clear glass smaller than the one below it, a sort of pyramid. This

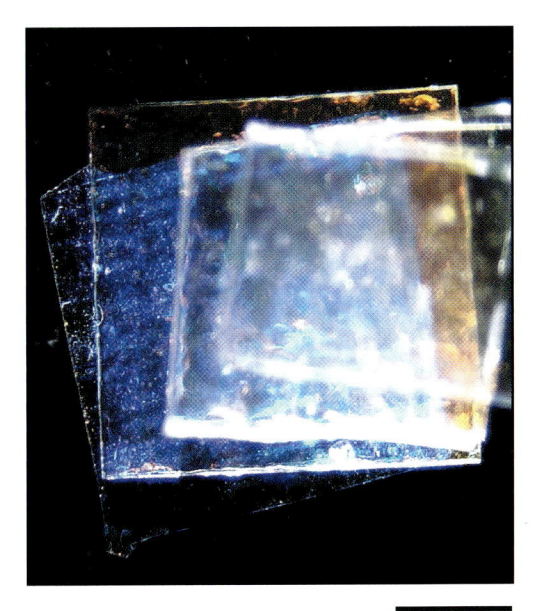

Photo 29

PHOTO 29
STACKED
DICHROIC
GLASS

Chapter 4

43

way, the spreading of the glass will be much more even, with the clear top and the black bottom staying pretty much together. I can't emphasize enough that only through hands-on experimentation are you going to learn to obtain the exact effect you are striving for.

The second change is the fusing temperature. If you've worked with hot glass at all, you know that "work" is a combination of time and temperature. You can ramp your kiln up quickly to your goal temperature for a short time, or you can heat your kiln to a lower temperature and let it soak (hold at that temperature) for a longer time. It is the latter which will give you a better result. The exact temperature you hold your glass at will depend on the softening temperature of the glass and how long you want to soak it. Let's say you decide to hold the kiln at 1475 degrees. Depending on the size of your glass stack and the internal dimensions of your kiln, you could get the results you want after an hour, more or less. It is the technique that is more important to describe here, rather than the exact parameters. It is the lower, slower temperature/time combinations which allow the glass and dichroic sandwich to pull itself apart, creating the crazes.

After the desired effect has been achieved, the kiln is allowed to cool and appropriate annealing procedures are taken. When the glass is cool, it can be cut and ground into smaller pieces if desired, then fire polished to completion.

Chapter 5

The Future of Dichroics in Glass Art

The use of dichroics in glass art is still in its infancy. Glassmaking has been around for thousands of years while dichroics first appeared in the glass industry a scant 20-25 years ago. Its lasting effect on the industry and on the art is yet to be seen. A hundred years from now, will interest have waned? Will future glass artists look back and view this 2-decade wave of excitement as just a fad? Or, are dichroics in glass art here to stay? Here are some thoughts from people involved in the manufacture of dichroic coatings as well as in the creation of the extraordinary glass art which utilizes them:

Linda Abbott, contributing editor, GLASScraftsman Magazine, artist and educator—"I think that dichroics will be a permanent fixture in glass art... I remember the first time I saw it. I was in Venice, California in the mid-70s. There was a little glass studio there, run part time by some aerospace guys. They were selling it for $25 a square inch. In the shop they had some pieces that were truly awful... but there was also a mobile that hung outside the door. As it turned, the colors changed and the reflection cast by the sunlight cast other colors on the street and on the building. Now THAT was spectacular. I managed to beg a scrap from these guys and carried it around with me in my pocketbook for many years. I would take it out almost every day and look at it. I absolutely cherished the stupid thing. Finally... the glass was available commercially and I could stop getting cut every time I looked for something in my pocketbook."

Glenn Brown, President, Austin Thin Films (creator of DichroMagic)—"We're busier now than we've been in several years... We're developing new machines to handle more and larger sheets of glass in an attempt to hold or even lower the price of the glass... I expect that art glass will always be about 70% of our dichroic production."

Dan Crow, Savoy Studios—"The biggest market is still fusing (for home decor) and jewelry, but I anticipate more and larger architectural designs using dichroic glass."

Dan Coursen, Engineer, Navitar Coatings (formerly, GM Vacuum Coatings)—"The use of dichroic glass is based on availability. As availability increases and becomes more affordable, more glass artists will be able to work with it. I also foresee an increase in architectural applications."

Peter McGrain, world renowned glass artist, speaker and author—"I believe dichroic glass is here for good, as a high-end sensational material for glass art. Nothing else has the dynamic visual impact of dichroic. Because of its inherent expense it is unlikely that dichroic glass will ever be overused and become cliche (as stained glass has, i.e. lampshades and door panels) through market over-saturation in low-end, fixture type applications. Like gold, there is no substitute, and the quality and value of work that integrates dichroic glass will remain high. Only the format of its use will vary and that is something to look forward to."

Gil Reynolds, acknowledged authority on fusing, and author of *The Fused Glass Handbook*, —referring to the future of dichroics, responded, "Bright!"

Gerald L. Sandberg, President, Coatings By Sandberg—"The future of Dichroic Glass is largely dependent upon the growth of the art industry in general as well as its inflow of new and aspiring artists. There also seems to be a growing surge of dichroic interest coming from the construction industry in the form of tile, wall, and other custom dichroic installations. The future of dichroic glass is also dependent upon customer knowledge of product, availability, and quality of product. This is why Coatings By Sandberg has standardized its high quality dichroic products, and CBS makes dichroic glass available to anyone who has a desire to work with glass. Furthermore, CBS strives to educate the artist population to help them make conscious decisions about the use of different types of medium available to express their innermost talents. With the talent, with the new blood, with the urge to stretch beyond one's capabilities, and with the motivation to push the frontier of art glass, dichroic glass will flourish."

John Williams, Pacific Glass—"The future is now. I anticipate more general acceptance by the public and more commercial applications. Dichroic glass is a natural progression. It's here to stay."

ANTICIPATING THE FUTURE

Predicting a bright future for dichroic coatings is a safe bet, if the activity of many of their manufacturers is any indication. Every company I spoke with is involved in building, expanding, retooling or evolving in some way. There are even indications that dichroic coated sheet prices are beginning to fall, due in part to these measures, as well as a healthy dose of good, old-fashioned competition. There are new shades, more textures, patterns with consistent color, dead-on uniformity of color across the entire sheet and more complex transmission/reflection combinations. The excitement of two decades ago hasn't waned, and as availability of dichroic glass increases, I believe that demand will continue to rise. More importantly, as glass artists gain an increased understanding of the way that dichroic coatings work, my hope is that they will feel more confident in experimenting with it, and in allowing their creative energies to lead them in new and constantly expanding directions.

This is an exciting time to be involved in the American Glass Movement. I was told recently that two hundred years from now historians and glass artists will look back and view the 1970s, 1980s and 1990s as an American Glass Renaissance— the same way we think of the artistic and cultural Renaissance in 15th and 16th century Europe. I have no doubt, if this prediction is true, that dichroics in glass art will have a prominent place in that history.

Gallery of Dichroic Glass

On the following pages are some examples of how dichroic glass is being used by some popular artists and designers working in glass and beading today.

Jackie Paciello-Truty

Ramses and Chariot

Ra

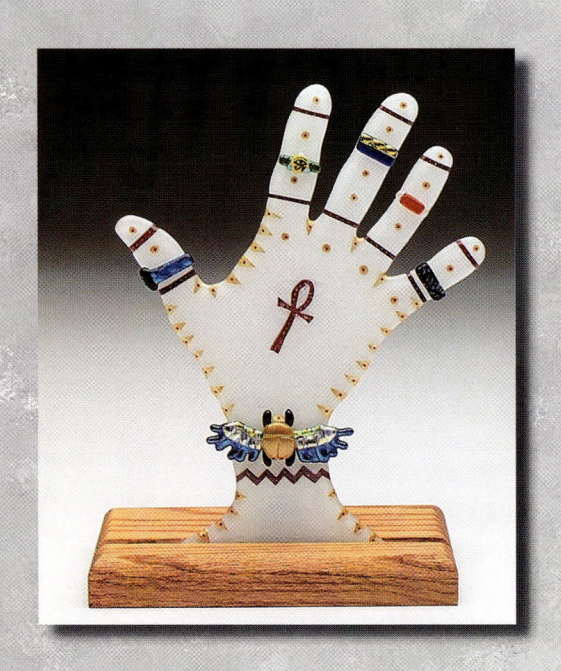

Hand of Fatima

Karen Stavert

Lampworked bead

Necklace

49

Nancy Geddes

Fused Dichroic Pins

Julie Rorden

Necklace

Rebecca Stewart

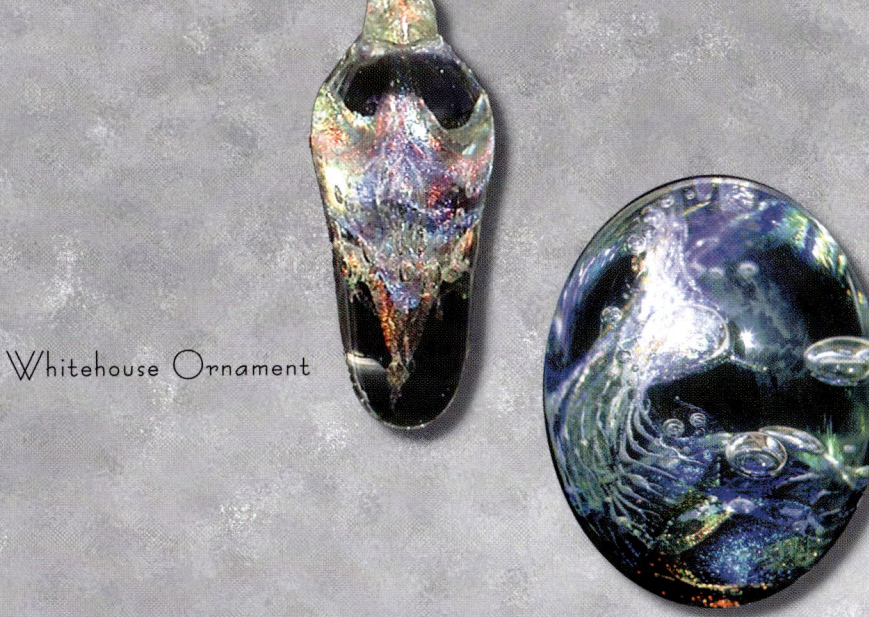

Whitehouse Ornament

Fire Opal World®

Leslie Videki

Green Dichroic Necklace

Newy Fagan

Migration

Manipulated Horse Series

Horse Panels

Leah Fairbanks

Lavender Urn with chunks of dichroic glass and gold.

Orchid Urn with patterned dichroic

Fall Leaves with chunks of dichroic

Howard Sandberg

Bowls - Fused with dichroic coated frit

Diane Demmitt

MX Bowl

Lilly's Bowl

Patricia Frantz

Lampworked Dichroic Beads

55

Linda Gettings/Janice Johnson

Leaf Fringe Fantasy

Night Sky

Green Dragon

Blue Moon

Janice Johnson

Amethyst Treasures

56

Debbye Simpson

Aquarium Cabochon

Silver Horse

Butterfly

Greenleaf

Landscape

Appendix A

Contributing Artists and Studios

Diane Demmitt
Orange, California
Page 56
Photographer: Howard Sandberg
Fused dichroic bowls

Newy Fagan
Newy Glassart Studio
Ocklawaha, Florida
Page 54
Top: *Migration,* Fused Dichroic Panels. 19" high x 52" wide
Photographer: Janice Hirmon
Middle: *Manipulated Horse Series*
Photographer: Ultra Vitrum
Bottom: Fused Dichroic *Horse* Panels
Photographer: Janice Hirmon

Leah Fairbanks
Willits, California
Pages 37 and 55
Photographer: George Post
Lavender Urn with chunks of dichroic glass and gold.
Orchid Urn with patterned dichroic
Fall Leaves with chunks of dichroic

Patricia Frantz
Patricia Frantz Studio
Page 57
Photographer: Patricia Frantz
Dichroic Beads

Nancy Geddes
Geddes Studio
Orangevale, California
Page 52
Photographer: Nancy Geddes
Fused Dichroic Pins

Linda Gettings
Center Valley, Pennsylvania
Page 58
Photographer: Heather Gogal Photography
Top left: Leaf Fringe Fantasy - beaded necklace with focal fused dichroic cabochon by Janice Johnson.
Top right: Night Sky - beaded necklace with focal fused dichroic cabochon by Janice Johnson.
Bottom left: Green Dragon - beaded necklace with focal fused dichroic cabochon by Janice Johnson.
Bottom right: Blue Moon - beaded necklace with focal fused dichroic cabochon by Janice Johnson.

Janice Johnson, Mrs. Magpie's
Allentown, Pennsylvania
Page 58
Photographer: Heather Gogal Photography
Amethyst Treasures - beaded necklaces with purple/wine fused dichroic cabochons

Peter McGrain
Bingen, Washington
Pages 33 and 35
Photographer: Peter McGrain
Page 33: *Good Exposure,* 1993. 20" x 14" Sandblasted and layered dichroic float glass, copper foil.
Page 35: *Monument,* 1995, Rochester International Airport, Rochester, NY. 25' x 100' Traditional stained glass, dichroic glass, bevels and jewels.

Jackie Paciello-Truty
Oak Lawn, Illinois
Page 50
Photographer: David Moll
Ramses & Chariot, 3' x 2' Stained Glass window created in copper foil with dichroic glass accents.
Ra, 14" x 18" Fused Dichroic Glass with beveled mirror.
Hand of Fatima, 8" x 6" Fused Glass with copper and dichroic glass.

Julie Rorden
Provo, Utah
Page 52
Photographer: Julie Rorden
Necklace - Dichroic cabochon set in silver with beaded rope.

Howard Sandberg
Orange, California
Page 56
Photographer: Howard Sandberg
Dichroic coated frit bowls

Debbye B. Simpson
Downers Grove, Illinois
Page 59
Photographer: David Simpson
Top left: *Aquarium*: Sandblasted dichroic glass over cathedral glass. Piece has been firepolished after sandblasting. Cabochon measures 2" x 1".
Top right: *Silverhorse:* Sandblasted dichroic glass with frit over opal glass. Cabochon measures 2" x 1".
Center: Butterfly: Sandblasted dichroic glass over black opal glass. Piece has been firepolished after sandblasting. Cabochon measures 1 3/4" x 1".
Bottom left: *Greenleaf*: Sandblasted dichroic glass over cathedral glass. Pendant measures 7/8" x 2".
Bottom right: *Landscape*: Sandcarved dichroic glass over cathedral glass. Cabochon measures 2" x 1".

Karen Stavert
Hot Glass Beads
Palm Beach Gardens, FL
Page 51
Photographer: David C. Miller - Hot Glass Beads
Top: Lampworked Dichroic Bead
Bottom: Necklace is sterling silver chain with the dichroic cabochons set into Art Clay Silver (which is fine silver).

Rebecca Stewart
R.Stewart Glass Blowing, Ltd
Portage, Michigan
Pages 37 and 53
Left: Christmas Ornament was created for the Blue Room Tree in the White House in 1997.
Right: Fire Opal World® was presented to First Lady Hillary Rodham Clinton at Buyers Market Of American Craft, Philadelphia, February 11, 1996. Worlds® are created by encasing multi-colored, dichroic glass within optically clear, soda-lime crystal. The artist forms and shapes the colored glass into various patterns that suggest both undersea and space themes.

Leslie Videki
Leslie Videki Designs
Traverse City, Michigan
Page 53
Dichroic Cabochon with beads

Appendix B

Charts of Comparative Codings

Company	Code	Transmitted	Reflected	Post Firing
Austin Thin Films	**Standard Colors**			
800 Paloma Dr. Suite 250	LY	Lt. yellow	violet	fades to dr. violet
Round Rock, TX 78664	YE	yellow	Dk. blue	violet
512-246-1122	AM	amber	bright blue	dk. blue
	PI	pink	turquoise	bright blue
	MA	magenta	teal	lt. blue/turqoise
	VI	violet	yellow/green	turqoise/teal
	BL	blue	yellow	teal to yellow/grn
	LB	lt. blue	gold	yellow
	CY	cyan	copper	gold
	RB	rainbow	rainbow	varies
	Premium Colors			
	GR	green	pink	lt.pink
	TE	teal	lt.pink	silver/golden pink
	TQ	turquoise	silver/pink	gold to green
	OR	orange	cyan	lt. blue
	RE	red	silver	cyan
	MR	yellow/grn	violet	bright magenta
	RR	clear	dk red	red/redorange
Coatings By Sandberg	**Standard Colors**			
856 N. Commerce St.	Y/V	yellow	violet	
Orange, CA 92867	Y/P	yellow	purple	
714-538-0888	Y/B	yellow	blue	
	P/T	pink	teal	
	M/G	magenta	green	
	B/G	blue	gold	
	C/C	cyan	copper	
	C/R	cyan	red	
	C/DR	cyan	dark red	
	C/DDR	cyan	dk. dk. red	
	RB1		rainbow1	
	Specialty Colors			
	R-Purple		purple	
	R-Salmon		salmon	
	R-Violet		violet	
	R-Emerald		emerald	
	R-CA-RED		candy apple	
	MX		mixture	
	Premium Colors			
	G/M	green	magenta	
	G/MB	green	magenta/blue	
	G/P	green	pink	
	R-Silver		silver	
	R/SB	red	silver/blue	
	RB2		rainbow2	

Company	Code	Transmitted	Reflected	Post Firing
GM Vacuum (Navitar Coating)	ART III Colors			
882 Production Place	Y/PR	yellow	purple	
Newport Beach, CA 92663-2810	Y/B	yellow	blue	Y/PR
949-642-5446	PK/T	pink	teal	Y/B
	M/GR	magenta	green	PK/T
	B/GD	blue	gold	M/GR
	CY/CP	cyan	copper	B/GD
	CY/R	cyan	red	CY/CP
	CY/DR	cyan	dark red	CY/R
	CY/DDR	cyan	red	CY/DR
	ART III Special Effects			
			Rainbow1	
			mixture	
	ART IV Colors			
		green	pink	
		green	magenta	
		red	silver	
			Rainbow2	
Savoy Studios	Standard Colors			
611 N. Tillamook St.	50	yellow	blue	
Portland, OR 97227	40	magenta	green/yellow	
503-282-5095	30	blue	gold	
	20	cyan	copper	
	10	clear	red	
	100	rainbow	rainbow	

Appendix C

Project: Art Clay Silver and Dichroic Glass

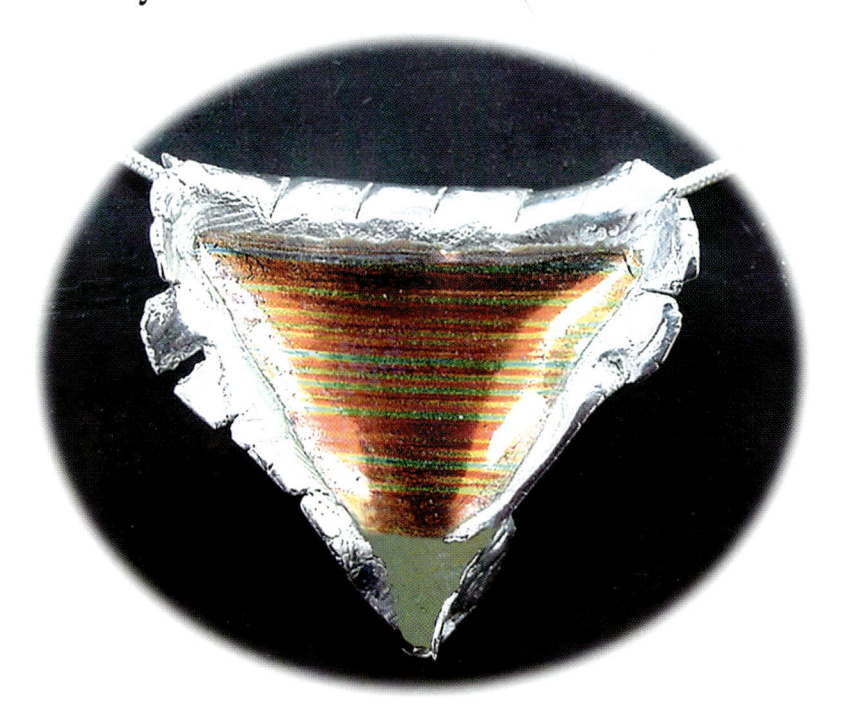

1) Cut your dichroic glass to the shape and size you want. Keep your piece under 1 ½" diameter. Remember that if you use one layer of glass, it will shrink slightly, and if you use more than 2 layers it will spread out slightly.

Use the piece of parchment or wax paper as a working surface. Take a drop or two of the olive oil and rub it into your palms. This will keep the silver clay from sticking to your hands. Take another drop and rub it very lightly over the working surface.

Open the Art Clay's outer Mylar package and the inner plastic wrap. Remove the clay and any excess that has stuck to the inner wrap. Roll the clay between your palms into a ball until smooth.

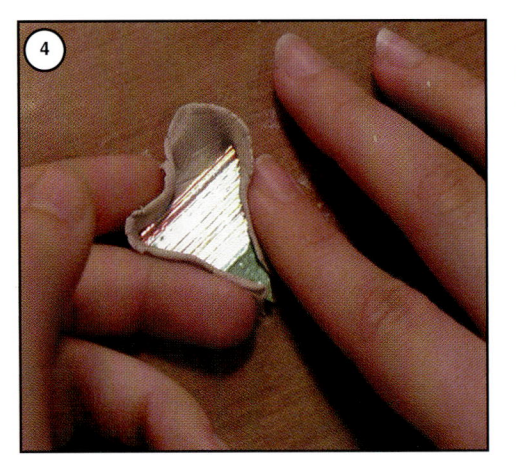

2) Place the ball on the working surface and, using the roller, roll the clay out into a long, rough oval. Check to make sure that it's long enough to go around the glass piece you've cut *(you can roll the clay over a textured surface, such as lace, brass texture plates, textured papers, etc.)*

3) Since Art Clay Silver begins to dry as soon as exposed to the air, dampen your small paintbrush with the water and lightly brush the edges and top of the clay. Be careful NOT to over-moisten.

Form the clay into a rough circle, molding to shape. If edges begin to dry and/or crack, brush again with a damp paintbrush.

4) Place the glass in the center so that approximately ¼" of one edge of the clay is tucked underneath the glass. Lift the other edge and create a freeform border around the glass, taking care not to cover more than ¼" of the outside perimeter of the glass with clay.

Where the clay ends meet, dab with water and press the ends together, sealing them. Make sure the Art Clay is not wrapped too tightly around the glass. Art Clay will shrink 8-10% during firing as the organic binders burn away, and if the glass is held too snugly prior to firing, the cooling and annealing process will cause the glass to crack.

5) Using the toothpick, roll the clay at the top of the piece back to form a bail (*this holds the chain*), and seal the clay to itself with a little water and pressure. There is no need to remove the toothpick. It will burn up in the kiln.

6) Using a hair dryer, or toaster oven (*set at 150 degrees*), or warming tray (*set to the same temperature*), dry the clay thoroughly. Any cracks or imperfections you want to fix prior to firing you can cover with a little clay mixed with water to create a paste (Art Clay Silver comes in a pre-mixed paste and syringe type as well).

7) Test the piece to make sure all of the moisture is gone by placing the hot piece on a metal surface. After 15-20 seconds, lift the piece and look for a cloud of condensation, which means there is still moisture trapped in the clay. If the piece is fired with moisture still present, the resulting steam and expansion of the water vapor may cause your piece to explode, crack or otherwise distort.

8) Once the piece is thoroughly dry, take out and file away rough spots, fine cracks and other imperfections. You can gather all the dust and filings and put them in a small film canister or other airtight container. All scraps of clay can be recycled by adding a little water and stirring until a paste is formed. This paste can be used as glue to attach clay pieces to clay pieces, or new clay to already fired silver pieces. As you can see, nothing is wasted!

Place the dried clay and glass piece in the kiln, either on a prepped or fiber paper-lined shelf. Use fiber blanket as needed to fill any open or suspended elements of the design.

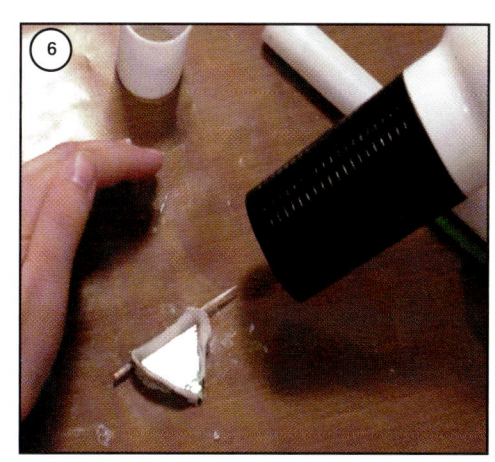

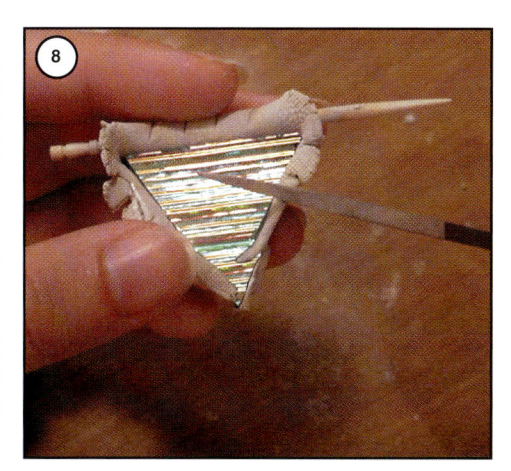

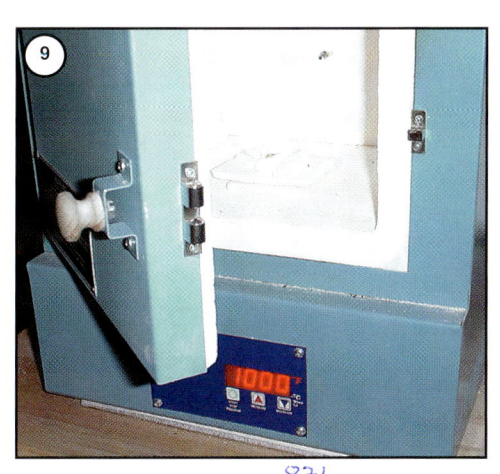

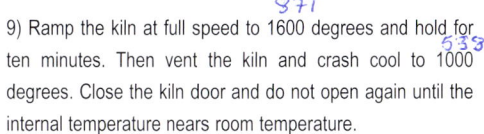

9) Ramp the kiln at full speed to 1600 degrees and hold for ten minutes. Then vent the kiln and crash cool to 1000 degrees. Close the kiln door and do not open again until the internal temperature nears room temperature.

10) When the completed piece is cool, use a steel or brass brush to remove the white oxidation coating that is left on the silver.

Finishing can be accomplished by using a burnishing tool, polishing cream or tumbling with stainless steel shot combined with water and jewelry cleaner. Your completed glass and silver piece is now ready to wear!

TOOL & SUPPLIES NEEDED

Dichroic coated black glass
Glass cutter
Grozing pliers
10 gm Art Clay Silver, clay type
Craft knife
Small paintbrush
Small container with water

Hair dryer, toaster oven or warming tray
Small (4" long) piece of ¾" PVC tubing as a roller
Two pieces matte board, 1"x 4" each
Plastic wrap and/or Ziploc Bag

Programmable kiln
Kiln-washed or fiber papered kiln shelf
Six inch square piece of baking parchment or wax paper
Few drops of olive oil
Toothpick

Other **GLASS PRESS** publications include:

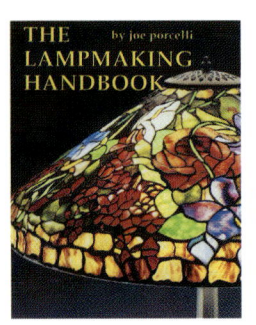

THE LAMPMAKING HANDBOOK
by Joe Porcelli
ISBN# 0-9629053-6-4
Build the ultimate stained glass project! Improve your lampmaking skills. Includes building a reproduction Tiffany lamp, designing a lamp, making templates and more. Still the *only* book on Lampmaking!!! In its 4th printing!

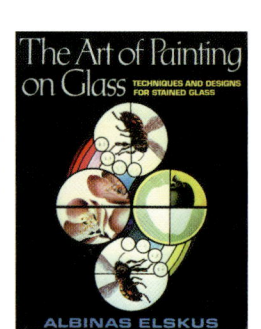

THE ART OF PAINTING ON GLASS
by Albinas Elskus.
ISBN# 0-9629053-0-5
The Bible of glass painting! Clearly written, illustrated reference on glass painting. Topics include: mixing colors, tools and equipment, tracing, matting, staining, enameling, etching, firing, and much, much more.

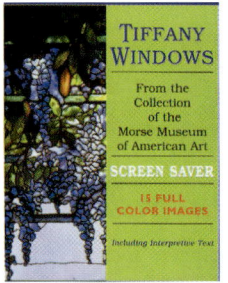

TIFFANY WINDOWS: Screen Saver
Louis Comfort Tiffany's home, Laurelton Hall was filled with some of the finest examples of his studios' creations. When the mansion burned in 1950 many of the windows were salvaged and are now in the collection of the Morse Museum of American Art in Winter Park, Florida. Windows from Laurelton Hall and others from the Morse Museum collection are reproduced in this beautiful full-color screen saver. (For PC's only!)

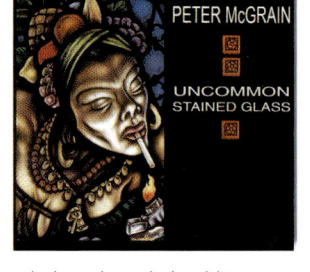

PETER McGRAIN: UNCOMMON STAINED GLASS
ISBN# 0-9629053-1-3
The life and artwork of one of today's most exciting stained glass artists.
"Peter McGrain is one of those few who has taken glass to levels rarely seen. His study and understanding of light and glass have helped him produce works of art that transcend the craft of stained glass".
- Gil Reynolds / Glass Artist / Educator

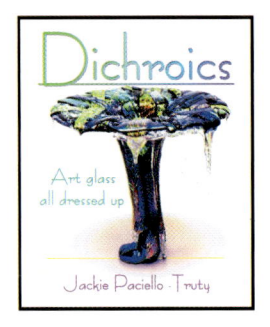

DICHROICS; Art Glass all Dressed Up
by Jackie Paciello-Truty
ISBN# 0-9629053-4-8
Dichroic-coated glass is fantastic. It is man-made, yet we are continually drawn to it; mesmerized by the play of light across and under its surface. Although developed in the laser industry, dichroic-coated glass found its way into the realm of creative expression. How is it created? How is it used in the Art Glass industry? How does it react to heat, light and layer? This book will provide insight and inspiration. Discover that the distance from the coldness of space to the heat of the kiln is shorter than you think.

**GLASS-ITECTURE:
The Style Handbook by Stu Goldman**
ISBN# 0-9629053-5-6
The portable, quick & easy guide to identifying period architectural and furnishing styles, and matching them with compatible stained glass motifs. Make educated observations, intelligent conversation and appropriate design suggestions... on site!

For more information visit us online at www.glasspress.com.